Managing Early Years Settings

Managing Early Years Settings

Supporting and Leading Teams

edited by

Alison Robins and Sue Callan

SAGE

Los Angeles • London • New Delhi • Singapore • Washington DC

First published 2009

SAGE Publications Ltd
1 Oliver's Yard
55 City Road
London EC1Y 1SP

SAGE Publications Inc.
2455 Teller Road
Thousand Oaks, California 91320

SAGE Publications India Pvt Ltd
B 1/I 1 Mohan Cooperative Industrial Area
Mathura Road
New Delhi 110 044

SAGE Publications Asia-Pacific Pte Ltd
33 Pekin Street #02-01
Far East Square
Singapore 048763

Library of Congress Control Number 2008926105

British Library Cataloguing in Publication data

A catalogue record for this book is available from the British Library

ISBN 978-1-84787-319-4
ISBN 978-1-84787-320-0 (pbk)

Typeset by C&M Digitals (P) Ltd., Chennai, India
Printed in Great Britain by TJ International, Padstow, Cornwall
Printed on paper from sustainable resources

Contents

About the Editors and Contributors

Editors

Alison Robins is a Senior Lecturer in the Centre for Early Childhood team within the Institute of Education at the University of Worcester and also works as an Associate Lecturer with the Open University. She is the coordinator of the Sector-endorsed Foundation Degree in Early Years and was involved in the development and validation of the degree, which currently runs at six partner institutions. Alison has taught in primary and middle schools, has been a SENCO and deputy head and has worked as a Teaching Assistant Training Officer for Worcestershire Local Authority. She is the editor of and a contributor to *Mentoring in the Early Years*, published by Sage in 2006.

Sue Callan has been a member of the collaborative partnership team for the Sector-endorsed Foundation Degree in Early Years at the University of Worcester for five years. She is a Senior Lecturer in the Centre for Early Childhood team within the Institute of Education at the University of Worcester and is responsible for the delivery of the programme in collaboration with Herefordshire Council Children's Services. Sue has been an adult education tutor for 18 years, specializing in community-based playwork and pre-school practice. She works with mature students in both personal tutor and mentor roles and is a contributor to *Mentoring in the Early Years,* published by Sage in 2006.

Contributors

Mandy Andrews is a Senior Lecturer in the Centre for Early Childhood team within the Institute of Education at the University of Worcester, teaching on the Early Years Professional Status routes, the National Professional Qualification for Integrated Centre Leadership, and undergraduate and postgraduate modules in Early Childhood. She was formerly Project Director of a large trailblazer Sure Start Local Programme and Early Designated Children's Centre in

Cornwall. Her research interests include both leadership concerns, and children's play and empowerment issues. Such interests arise from both her academic qualification in Public and Social Administration, and her earlier employment as a local authority Children's Play Officer. Mandy has been teaching playwork and leadership skills to adults for over a decade.

Natalie Canning is a Senior Lecturer at University College Plymouth, St Mark and St John. She is Programme Leader for the Foundation Degree in Early Years (Child Development) and teaches across a variety of early childhood undergraduate and postgraduate programmes. Previously, she worked at the University of Worcester and on overseas childcare projects. Her background is in playwork and social work, particularly supporting children to explore their social issues through play. She has undertaken research in the area of children's empowerment in play and is particularly interested in children's play dispositions.

Alison Morrall has worked with children and families in various contexts for over 25 years. She is currently tutoring for the Learning Skills Council in Herefordshire. Alison also delivers training to early years practitioners, assessing the delivery of the Language and Play programme within a variety of settings throughout Powys. She holds a BA (Hons) Degree in Integrated Early Childhood Studies, and is presently studying for a MSc in Educational Management and Leadership.

Janet Murray is a Principal Lecturer and Head of the Centre for Early Childhood within the Institute of Education at the University of Worcester. She leads a multi-professional team delivering undergraduate and postgraduate Early Childhood programmes. She has been a tutor on the National Professional Qualification in Integrated Centre Leadership since the national roll-out in 2005 and she has a professional and academic background in health and education management as well as early years teaching. Janet has worked in the public and private sector in the UK and abroad. She contributed to *Mentoring in the Early Years,* published by Sage in 2006.

Melanie Pilcher is the Policy and Standards Manager for the Pre-School Learning Alliance and has worked in early years and childcare for nearly 20 years. She is studying for a MSc in Educational

Management and Leadership and previous roles include nursery manager, childcare development officer, college lecturer, early years trainer and mentor. Previous collaborations include a chapter in *Mentoring in the Early Years*, edited by Alison Robins in 2006 and published by Sage.

Michael Reed qualified as a primary teacher gaining postgraduate qualifications in educational psychology and inclusive education. He held senior positions in schools and early years settings. He has worked in the private sector involved in educational training and consultancy and now works part-time as a Senior Lecturer in the Centre for Early Childhood team within the Institute of Education at the University of Worcester. He is also an Associate Lecturer with the Open University and has written course materials for the OU Foundation Degree. He teaches on undergraduate and postgraduate programmes, the Foundation Degree in Early Years and the National Professional Qualification in Integrated Centre Leadership. He has written a number of publications and articles and has a particular interest in management and leadership.

Acknowledgements

The editors would like to acknowledge the work of all contributors to this text and the practioners who have provided insights into practice. This must include Nicki Ovel, Cath Davenport, Viv Daly, Alison Murphy, Jude Simms, Carole Ellis and Claire Richards. Thanks must also go to Jude Bowen and Amy Jarrold at Sage Publications for their enthusiasm and assistance throughout this project.

We would also like to thank all the staff, children and parents at the Green Croft Children's Centre, Hereford for allowing us to take the photographs used throughout and John Lusardi for his photographic skills.

This book is written for the dedicated and highly motivated early years professionals and the children and families with whom they work.

Alison Robins and Sue Callan

Introduction

Janet Murray, Alison Robins and Sue Callan

By being grounded in practice, this book aims to meet the needs of those facing the challenges currently presented by *Every Child Matters* (DfES, 2004a) *The Children's Workforce Strategy* (DfES, 2005a) and *The Children's Plan* (DCSF, 2007), to work together in a new way for the benefit of young children and families. The content of this book applies as much to those working as childminders as to leaders of Children's Centres, and it is a useful resource for those studying to achieve Early Years Professional Status (EYPS) and the National Professional Qualification in Integrated Centre Leadership (NPQICL). It also serves students and tutors of Early Years degrees (Level 5 and 6) and practitioners, governors or parents with an interest in early years leadership and management, whatever type of setting is within their experience.

Throughout the text, links are made with current standards and policy, for example, standards for EYPS and NPQICL and the themes within the Early Years Foundation Stage (EYFS), and their application within an early years leadership and management context. In a practical sense, the book focuses on theoretical perspectives linked directly to the views of practitioners who enact change. These are set out as 'pictures of practice' alongside academic arguments and evidence from published research provided by the contributors. In essence, the text moves away from purely theoretical perspectives towards developing practice. An underlying premise is that children and families are at the heart of early years services and therefore the current government's ambition to bring about a transformation of the sector involves all who are associated and affected by it. As a consequence, when referring to 'teams', children and their families are considered to be part of this team. Although this book is designed to support those involved in and affected by current government policy and initiatives, the intention is that the ideas and arguments can be applicable in changing circumstances, whatever their nature.

The enormity of changes experienced within the early years sector across the four nations of the United Kingdom in recent years is highlighted by Moyles (2006), in the introduction to her publication *Effective Leadership and Management in the Early Years*. She provides a thought-provoking scenario which asks us to think about the people who, without any formal training or qualifications, have found themselves undertaking leadership and management roles in private or voluntary settings which are becoming increasingly complex businesses. She gives an example which will be familiar to many of our readers, of 'the playgroup leader, a mother of young children, who suddenly found herself responsible for, amongst other things ... ensuring staff within the setting received opportunities for professional development' (Introduction). This is not an uncommon experience and even where formal training has been undertaken, leadership and management have not generally been central elements of early years qualifications at any level. This situation is changing with the growing recognition that there is a significant relationship between the quality of a setting and its leadership. The drive to raise quality of service and workforce across the sector needs to attend to the development of leadership and management, and more opportunities are occurring to study leadership and management in initial training and professional development courses. This book intends to support such courses by reflecting the particular nature of the sector and the context of the learner, providing reflective activities which are transferable and relevant to the workplace.

This book aims to contribute to the developing knowledge concerning leadership and management practice across the early years sector with the primary focus on leading people and managing the development of practice in order for individuals to become agents of change. A unique feature of the book is that each chapter considers the impact of leadership and management of settings on the children and their families. With this in mind, the contributors hope to inspire practitioners to take ownership of the lead role and regard such management as fundamental to the well-being of the community.

The sentiment expressed by Roger Gill that 'seeking the answer to the question "what is leadership?" is like searching for the Holy Grail' (Gill, 2006: 8) indicates the complexity and variety of perspectives on the subject. The relationship between leadership and management is open to debate and this book does not seek to provide a definitive answer or suggest that we could arrive at such a position. There are a wide range of theories and models which contribute to our overall understanding of leadership and management and the contributors to this book will draw upon competing perspectives within their chapters. We do believe, however, that the real value of considering the theories surrounding leadership and management is in the potential to move forward our understanding of experiences in practice. This does not simply mean using the models which fit comfortably within our personal contexts but those which challenge our assumptions and which we can use critically to evaluate our working knowledge in practice. This book assumes a readiness of the reader to engage in reflection in order to apply, evaluate, contest and review theory and principles of practice within their own context to come to a greater understanding and informed ways of working. In this spirit, it is worthwhile the reader spending a few moments identifying their own perspective on leadership and management and reflecting upon the possible origins of and influences on their own thinking.

In considering conventional ways in which the terms leadership and management are used, there is a danger of confusing attributes with roles and functions or just considering one of these aspects. Attempts at drawing distinctions between leadership and management include a straightforward division between operational (micro) and strategic (macro) skills and functions, with the former seen as the province of management and the latter as leadership. Sometimes it is the tasks undertaken which are seen as differentiated, with management tasks being pragmatic or technical and associated with running an efficient organization, whereas leadership provides the human dimension, the world of workplace relationships and interaction (Morgan, 1986). Leadership may also be seen as providing the wherewithal to motivate and mobilize human resources to work towards goals (Rodd, 2006). Some attempts to differentiate between the terms evoke more emotive distinctions, for example, managing as coping and leadership as inspiring or initiating (Smith & Langston, 1999). This could affect attitudes and perceptions and have implications for the way we see ourselves and those with whom we work. Would you prefer to be seen as someone who copes or who inspires? It is therefore important that the two terms are not given prejudicial or negative connotations which suggest one is more valued than the other. In seeking clarification of terminology, we do not want to draw too much separateness. Stark distinctions might not be the most helpful as leading and managing need to interrelate. 'Managers may be good at *managing* and nominally regarded as leaders, but the most effective managers exercise *effective leadership*' (Gill, 2006: 10).

The nature of leadership and management within the field of early years is undoubtedly that of a human dimension. Human resources and human development are the essence of the business, not the technical efficiency and outputs associated with industry, so it is not helpful to see management as technical, nor just as the utilization of human resources. 'Effective leadership in the early childhood profession is about working towards creating a community and providing a high quality service' (Rodd, 2006: 24). Early years leaders and managers work in the world of relationships and need to lead people. This is not to say that leadership is confined to recognized positions of authority such as the manager. Leadership can be diffused within the organization, among staff, governors, parents and children, any of whom can initiate change and improvement, motivate and enthuse others, contribute to developing the direction and mission of the setting, and model and communicate its values and ethos (Jones & Pound, 2008). Gill (2006) sees leadership as both extrinsic (provided by another) and intrinsic (from within ourselves), where individuals have vision, are self-aware and self-driven. Whether extrinsic or intrinsic, leadership 'creates a sense of direction, empowerment and the motivation we feel when we are doing or achieving something worthwhile' (Gill, 2006: 11). This concept of leadership fits well with early years as a community service, whether public or privately owned, as the organization has a moral purpose in improving outcomes for children and families.

This view of leadership in the early years sector means that the contents of this book could be relevant and useful across the myriad types of settings and stakeholders, including childminders, parents and governors, students and team leaders, all of whom can exert leadership influence and who have a vested interest in the quality of early years provision.

The Aim of the Book

The aim of this book is to support the reader in exploring contemporary views on how interprofessional leadership and management skills can be part of the process of meeting the needs of families, as well as managing resources and enhancing teamwork within a wide range of early years settings. The contributors acknowledge that there are similarities and differences between the four nations in terms of their approaches to early years but this text is written within the context of policy and legislation in England. The general principles, however, and experiences within practice which are discussed, are applicable across all settings within the UK.

Overall, the chapters provide the reader with a mixture of relevant theory, practical suggestions, pictures of practice, questions for reflection and discussion (pauses for thought), activities for personal and professional development and suggestions for further reading. Each chapter finishes with questions or thoughts that may be used individually, as part of a team, or by a tutor or mentor in order to reflect upon personal and professional development planning. We do not wish to impose any particular structure or approach to this activity but hope that by considering and reflecting upon these questions or thoughts that understanding, values and beliefs underpinning practice will continue to develop. The contributors hope that this book provides the reader with the means to a greater understanding of practice, future aims, prompts for further action and exploration of thinking. Above all, we hope this book supports strong relationship building among a community of learners in whatever team and context.

Content

This book leads the reader towards a view of leadership and management that encompasses a value-based, principled approach. Chapter 1 identifies the need to take into account the nature and characteristics of early years, the influence this might have, and the demands it might make, on the leadership and management of settings in following a principled approach. The text also emphasises, in Chapter 2, the importance of recognizing the value of individual contributions within an early years setting, and explores how leaders empower others to support the development and sustainability of the setting in its approach to working with children, families and communities. Chapter 3 moves the reader forward and explores the nature of change in early years settings. It considers how leaders in those settings can draw upon their understanding of pedagogical practices to inform their change management skills and develop a 'change embracing' organization.

Chapter 4 considers the way that management and leadership needs to be concerned with various professional groups working together to support children and families and explores what we mean by 'professionals working in partnership'. In Chapter 5, group dynamics and the facilitation of team-building to encourage the development of positive motivation and attitudes is considered, alongside potential difficulties and the importance of emotional literacy for the effective operation of teams. Chapter 6 explores the notion of supporting teams using a variety of mentoring techniques and considers why and how the skills used by a mentor are an important part of leadership, the management of change, and an essential element of working effectively with children and their families. Finally, Chapter 7 focuses on the context, literature and professional principles underpinning work with parents and encourages a reflective approach to work in settings. As a result, this chapter is a working case study with which to plan for professional development needs and improvement action in teams.

Clarification and explanation of some of the terms used throughout this book can be found in the Glossary. Where practitioners have drawn on experiences, care has been taken to respect and preserve confidentiality and deal ethically with privileged information.

1

Value-based Leadership and Management

Janet Murray

Chapter Overview

This chapter considers the nature and characteristics of early years provision and the influence this might have, and demands it might make, on the leadership and management of settings. The opening section explains the development of diverse provision in the sector, putting some of the leadership and management challenges into context. Subsequent sections explore concepts integral to the nature of early years and their significance for leadership and management. The need for a value-based, principled approach to leading and managing is proposed, in order to provide a firm foundation for ethical decision-making which keeps the interests of the child and family at the heart of the operation of the organization.

Characteristics of the Early Years Sector – the Development of Diverse Provision

The early years sector in Britain, and England in particular, is the inheritance of political disinterest stemming from a cultural, economic and political divide between what constitutes public and private interests of the state and the individual in matters of childcare and education. During the development of the Welfare State, early childhood was seen as the province and prime responsibility of the family rather than the state. The foundations of the current school education system were laid in 1870 with the Elementary Education

Act. This established an arbitrary starting age of five years which subsequently became compulsory with publicly funded state school education and created a divide between care and education which still persists. Throughout the 20th century, national policy and resources were largely focused on the requirements of state education, resulting in years of political and economic neglect for childcare and early education. Changing social, cultural, economic and employment trends during the 20th century increased demand for childcare outside the immediate or extended family, and the absence of a publicly funded entitlement and concomitant regulation allowed a mixed economy of provision to grow rapidly in the Private, Voluntary, and Independent (PVI) sector to meet the demand and space left by a lack of national policy and funding. As political interest to increase access to early education and childcare developed in the late 1990s, Meeting the Childcare Challenge (DEE, 1998) set out the National Childcare Strategy and economic initiatives were developed around the existing pattern of provision, further embedding the market economy in the sector. Increased public funding brought regulation and national standards in the attempt to bring some comparability and assurance of quality between the diverse types of provision, yet the sector remained fragmented and characterized by variety in types of settings and the services they offer, the level of staff qualifications and ratios of staff to children. It can be argued that a range of provision arising from the operation of market forces offers choice and the potential to meet individual or community requirements but it sets challenges in respect of equity, access and affordability as well as quality, continuity and coherence of service. As Dahlberg and Moss (2005) suggest, the operation of market forces gives the appearance of devolution and the rhetoric of diversity and choice but with a consequent imbalance of provision. Successive governments have sought to redress this by regulation, standardization, subsidy and funded programmes targeted at the most disadvantaged.

Since the political spotlight turned onto the early years sector during the late 20th century, there has been a flurry of activity in relation to policy and legislation, creating a driving force to raise quality within this complex and diverse sector and working towards more commonality and integration of services, a theme extended in Chapter 4. Persistent distinctions between childcare and education have inhibited development of a unified service and a powerful professional voice to gain recognition of the issues facing the early years sector. Dahlberg and Moss (2005) argue that the end result of the British approach is a system which is less dynamic and capable of change when compared with Sweden over the last 40 years. In light of the recent policy and strategy initiatives, which are demanding transformation of the sector into a more unified and integrated whole, this judgement will need to be deferred until their success can be properly assessed.

The Five Year Strategy for Children and Learners (DfES, 2004b) set out the first long-term policy ambitions and direction for the sector, and Every Child Matters (DfES, 2004c) expressed a vision and intention for developing integrated, seamless services. The Childcare Act (2006) and the Early Years Foundation Stage (EYFS) (DfES, 2007a) bring care and early education closer together in a single statutory framework. The government's agenda for change intends to be transformative, as indicated by the statement of the Secretary of State for Children, Schools and Families in the foreword to the Children's Plan: 'this Children's Plan is the beginning of a new way of working' (DCSF, 2007).

The history of development of early years provision in Britain, however, leaves a legacy of separation of childcare from education and distinction between education as a public good and childcare as a private commodity, which will take time and more than legislation to overcome. History has a pervading influence on the values and beliefs of the policy makers, service providers and service users, and a legacy which affects the composition and nature of the workforce and the people who lead and manage early years settings. There is a predominance of private providers and reliance on unqualified assistance, qualifications at lower levels than for teaching, and persisting low status and a largely female workforce. Initiatives such as Early Years Professional Status (EYPS) are working towards achieving graduate-level leaders of practice in the PVI sector but contain no organizational leadership or management element.

We are currently experiencing unprecedented levels of funding to raise qualification levels in the non-maintained sector (aptly named Transformation Funds, succeeded by Graduate Leader Fund), particularly for leaders of practice through EYPS, and public investment in the training of Children's Centre Leaders, through the National Professional Qualification in Integrated Centre Leadership (NPQICL). These initiatives aim to cultivate the leadership skills required to meet the challenges of change, expansion and integration relating to professional practice and organizational and community development.

The Public Accounts Committee (House of Commons, 2007) indicated a need to raise qualifications, skills and confidence of staff (including managers), as only a third of 134 Children's Centre staff interviewed by the National Audit Office felt well qualified to perform their roles. The challenge for leadership across the early years sector is immense and requires confident, capable and creative managers. Yet the sector is largely untrained in management and its managers have been weighed down by the emphasis on accountability and regulation, leaving little room for the constructive contesting of practice.

Picture of Practice

Kim is a pre-school supervisor in a voluntary setting catering for children from age two to 'rising' five years. She is a trained primary teacher and has worked at the pre-school for ten years. She was promoted to supervisor after three years.

'The supervisor left for financial reasons and she asked me to take over running the group. I agreed as there was no one else to do it but said to the staff that we would do it together, as I had no more experience than they did at managing a pre-school.

Our motivations for working there were very similar in the beginning: convenience of the location and pre-school operating hours, pending or supplementing another job. None were trained in early years.

I hadn't expected to stay. I didn't actually choose to become an early years leader. From talking informally to colleagues from other settings, their experiences were similar. Many said, "I don't know how it happened really – I was just in the right place at the right time and have ended up staying!"

I agreed to accept the job as supervisor at the pre-school because they had asked me; my teaching degree allowed me to work at a supervisory level; my children were at the pre-school, so this allowed me to be involved in their education and I didn't have to pay for their fees whilst I worked there, saving money and I needed the small amount paid in wages.

Kim is accountable to the management committee but has no professional manager. All the staff members are part-time, with variable hours. Kim has just completed EYPS and feels that there is a need to change some aspects of practice but believes this will need the staff to change and that this could be difficult. They are not keen to undergo training and Kim finds herself using Ofsted as a 'stick' to force a change in established routines.

Inevitably, differences in settings affect the nature of provision, organizational goals, services offered, and the experience for the child and family. The nature of the organization impacts on leadership and management issues, dilemmas, drivers and constraints. Leaders and managers in the sector come from diverse backgrounds with varying levels of experience and training in early years and management. So it is important when considering leadership and management in the early years that we do not fall into the trap of thinking that we are dealing with a single entity and recognize that the challenges faced in different aspects of the sector may have distinctive features. This does not mean that commonalities cannot be identified but that complexity and diversity need to be acknowledged as part of the challenge. It is unlikely that 'one size fits all' in terms of leadership and management approaches. The history and characteristics of current provision in the sector, together with the agenda for transformative change, provide the essential background and context in which to consider the leadership and management of early years settings. If we are to face the challenge and deal with diversity, a flexible approach to leading and managing will be required but it is important that it is leadership which suits the nature of early years.

The Nature of Early Years – Pedagogy and Moral Purpose

'The term pedagogy is seldom clearly defined' (Mortimore, 1999: 228), but effective pedagogy is fit for purpose in that the teaching approach, the learning purposes, and conditions for learning suit the needs of the learner, whether child or adult, and promote their personal learning and development. All participants in the early years context can be seen as learners, whether children, parents and carers, staff team members, managers or governors. They are all contributors to the development of the organization and the individuals and groups associated with it. The pedagogic orientation of early years is on learning to learn within a social context. In this sense, the early years setting is a community with a collective interest in promoting the process of learning and creating the conditions in which children can thrive and so help to secure the well-being of future generations. Sergiovanni (2001) draws attention to the link between pedagogy and leadership (from the Greek derivation of the term pedagogy): 'leadership in the learning community has a special meaning that comes from the word pedagogy' (2001: 72) and involves caring, supporting and guiding.

'Without a concept like pedagogy, which starts from the assumption that care and education are inextricably intertwined, it has proven difficult to conceptualize and practise an integrated approach to early childhood services' (Dahlberg & Moss, 2005: 130). Yet integration is now at the heart of policy direction and strategy for services for young children and families, and the concept of pedagogy is gaining renewed interest as a cultural, professional force which could be harnessed to support integration. 'Cultural forces rely on common purposes, values, commitments, and norms that result in relationships among people that have moral overtones, relationships that ensure caring and inclusiveness' (Sergiovanni, 2001: 103). Pedagogy underpins professional practice and is based on a complex interaction of values, beliefs and theory interpreted through experience. If pedagogy is a potential unifying mechanism for the sector, the assumptions and underlying values need to be explored to arrive at a greater understanding of its fundamental nature.

Roger Smith argues that values permeate and influence all aspects of policy and practice in children's services, 'from strategic decisions, through management, planning and decision-making, to the critical point at which interventions are actually put into operation' (2005: 1), and therefore the ability to reflect on values and understand the way they can shape policy and practice is a necessary skill. He warns against any expectation that this will lead directly to solutions for problems or dilemmas in service provision but, nevertheless, believes that a heightened appreciation of the link between values and practice can support decision-making strategies. If we take this link between values, practice and management further, there is a case for developing reflective leadership practice based on the principles of early years pedagogy. A deepening consciousness of the values and principles of early years practice can then be used to inform and influence leadership thinking and action in strategic and operational development – a theme extended in Chapter 3.

Understanding the nature, purpose and values at the heart of an organization or service is not just helpful but essential for those who have a leadership and management responsibility. Drucker (1999) stresses the importance of sufficient compatibility between individual and service values and the need for self-knowledge to recognize where there are tensions between personal and organizational values:

'to work in an organization the value system of which is unacceptable to a person, or incompatible with it, condemns the person both to frustration and to non-performance' (Drucker, 1999: 176). It is particularly important, therefore, at a time of rapid and transformative change in early years to develop the capacity for examining values both individually and collectively.

Sharing values connects people in meaningful and productive relationships

 Activity

Recognizing your own value position

Take a few moments to consider: what matters to you in working with young children? What do you hold dear and why? Who or what has influenced you in forming these values?

- What matters?
- Why? (beliefs)
- What are your influences (or formative experiences)?

Transformational change is radical. It challenges established practices and creates stressful situations (Rodd, 2006), requiring great resourcefulness and skilful human understanding from those in leadership or management positions to navigate the team safely and constructively towards a new and improved service. Roger Smith (2005) places the role of values as central in the provision of children's services because of their powerful motivating effect. Where individual practice values and wider principles underpinning social policy coincide, such as children's rights, a powerful force for committed action is created. The converse is also true where unresolved, conflicting agendas compete and undermine the process of policy implementation and organizational development. Many different value positions, interest groups and power bases are at play within individual settings and across children's services. An artificial distinction between care and education is one such value position which can be divisive or inhibit collegiality and common purpose, if left unaddressed. Michael Fullan (1999) recognizes the challenge such diversity presents in achieving moral purpose, which he defines as 'making a positive difference in the lives of all citizens' (1999: 11) and identifies the need for empathy, relationship building, interaction and the creation of mutual interests to encourage collaborative cultures with a commitment to the greater good.

The early years sector carries with it a social responsibility and ethic of care for the most vulnerable member of our society, the young child. A strong sense of public service and belief in the ultimately beneficial purpose of the organization creates and sustains commitment and perseverance. Fullan suggests that, 'in post-modern society, more than ever before, a strong commitment to the role of moral purpose in educational reform is crucial' (1999: 1). A firm belief in the individual and collective ability to make a contribution which will make a difference to the lives of children and families can inspire and sustain early years practitioners, leaders and managers through difficult periods. In this respect, leadership is crucial, as it 'creates a sense of direction, empowerment and the motivation we feel when we are doing or achieving something worthwhile' (Gill, 2006: 11). A commitment to the moral purpose of the organization can provide leaders with motivation in the face of adversity, through the peaks and troughs of change and the frustrations and limitations of changing policy and resource allocation. Denhardt et al. (2002) also note this steadfast commitment as a necessary trait of the effective public service sector manager. In the context of early years settings, however, this is not a trait that can reside only in the public sector or in a single setting or in the designated manager alone. Understanding and interpretation of moral purpose needs exploring and nurturing at local level and among teams, if commitment to improving outcomes for children and families is to be sustained. This applies particularly during a period of policy change which is seeking transformation of the sector and where the drive for raising quality and providing seamless integrated services affects the whole workforce. Values influence professional practice and commitment, and therefore a principal leadership quality and function is to draw out individual values and develop a shared service commitment in others, nurturing and fostering belief in their capacity and ability to make a valuable contribution, ensuring that each contribution is recognized.

Picture of Practice

As an early years practitioner, Kim is committed to personal and professional development. She has taken steps to ensure this for herself. After the first year of settling into the new role of supervisor, she increasingly broadened her interests beyond her own setting. She began to take part in county-wide working parties, hosted Good Practice sessions in her setting on behalf of the county Early Years Team and gained commissions for writing articles for national pre-school magazines. She enrolled on EYPS and a Masters course in Early Childhood: 'As I became more and more aware of the early years world beyond my setting, I developed opinions about government policy and initiatives.' Her personal learning made her more conscious of the beliefs underpinning her practice and increased her commitment and determination to develop that understanding in her team.

Her initial assessment was that staff needed to take professional development courses to create greater understanding of theory in order to make changes in practice. She valued formal courses because of her own successful experience and was frustrated by her team colleagues who seemed disinterested or unwilling to go on courses. Disagreements developed over practice, which turned into cliques and divisions in workplace relationships which were becoming destructive. Kim observed deterioration in children's behaviour and began to consider if the underlying causes were staff behaviour and relationships. She conducted appraisals which revealed feelings of not being valued, lack of confidence which led to feeling threatened, and feelings of being usurped by more qualified but less experienced staff.

The revelations of the appraisals have led her to recognize that if she is to change practice, she firstly needs to address the emotional climate of the workplace by discovering what matters to individual staff and showing appreciation of their abilities to contribute based on current skills, in order to raise confidence, competence, and commitment to a shared sense of purpose.

(Continued)

(Continued)

I wanted to make each staff member feel that they were making a positive contribution and that their efforts were important to the quality of the provision. I asked each member of staff to do something to improve the experience for the children based on what they had told me during appraisals or chats or what I knew about their interests and strengths. I was thinking about how you would get the children to learn and thought that you would start with what they knew, liked, and could do already. To create a community of learners amongst the staff I wanted to do the same thing. It has made me reflect on what I mean by a learner. Is it academic pursuit, or could it also mean knowing yourself, your strengths and weaknesses and how the children should learn too?

In this scenario, Kim sought to discover what her team valued in children's learning and in their own area of expertise. She appealed to their sense of moral purpose (to improve the experience of the children) to put this into effect by taking on a negotiated responsibility matched to their interest and expertise, thereby increasing their motivation, commitment and belief in their own ability to make a contribution. She applied principles of early years pedagogy to the leadership of her team by listening, valuing the diversity of individual qualities, starting from what they can do and giving ownership, responsibility and accountability for what they do. She has since checked periodically with the team about their progress and their feelings regarding their new responsibility and a much happier working atmosphere has been observed. For Kim, this is just the beginning of building a culture of learning and responsibility which equips her team and her own leadership of it to take on the challenges of change in the sector.

'Negative cultures are debilitating' (Fullan, 2005: 26), whereas positive cultures are empowering and are based on shared values and beliefs with sufficient common ground over what is important to maintain focus on the direction of collective action, while permitting individual flexibility within it. Sergiovanni (2001: 103), talking in the context of schools, emphasized the need for people to be bound together in 'a common moral quest', forming a community with shared purposes and values which give the school a cultural identity and the participants a sense of belonging and involvement. He argues that this connects people in meaningful and productive relationships in which they care for and nurture each other, in a bonded fellowship which engenders a moral commitment and mutual responsibility.

Point for Reflection

Consider the view that there is a moral purpose in working in the early years setting. How would you express your own 'moral purpose'? To what extent do you think this is a common quest within a setting known to you/between different types of settings?

List ways in which you have felt a sense of belonging and involvement in a group and list things that have helped to forge that identity.

An explicit value base can both determine and provide a reasoned basis for practice in an early years setting and this applies to leadership and management practice as much as to professional pedagogical practice. A common and shared core of values which underpin the organization's operating principles provides a reference point to enable the early years manager to act visibly with integrity and employ leadership approaches which provide order and direction for systems, procedures, decision-making and everyday practice, even in the face of conflicting pressures and interests. It can provide early years managers with a compass to guide the route of service development and enhancement and help determine how that route is navigated. A single and predominant value position can, however, have serious limitations in that it restricts the ability to assess specific contextual factors which require different priorities and judgments regarding which values take precedence in different circumstances. Disagreements are to be expected and welcomed, otherwise staff relations are built on compliance and practice is unquestioned, but conditions need to be created for constructive openness in exploring different viewpoints. 'If they (leaders) show an inflexible commitment to a vision – even if it is based on passionate moral purpose – they can drive resistance underground and miss essential lessons until it is too late' (Fullan, 2005: 72). In this context, Fullan is talking about one level of leadership but conflict is met at every level and needs to be positively handled to be productive. The ability to recognize one's own value position and assess competing perspectives and their potential impact is necessary for rational decision-making. 'Successful organizations explicitly value differences and do not panic when things go wrong' (Fullan, 2005: 72). Diversity can add strength in complex situations if coupled with effective communication and positive relationships, as it encourages team development of shared and explicit value statements which are recognized as relative and sometimes competing. This can support the early years manager and team in dealing with dilemmas, being steadfast in pursuit of goals, being accountable for their actions and decisions and reviewing and learning after reflecting on the outcomes.

A value-based approach to managing early years settings supports the daily pragmatic functions and operations in which tensions arise between competing, and sometimes conflicting, pressures, drivers and interests such as children's interests and parents' wishes, financial constraints, the regulatory framework and curriculum requirements. The profit orientation of the private sector, for example, could be considered to be in direct conflict with putting the needs of children first. However, the tension between financial resource allocation and the quality of experience for the child is certainly not a value conflict restricted to the private sector! Such tensions exist regardless of the type of early years organization, whether private, voluntary, independent, or state-maintained, but, ultimately, no early years organization will survive if it ignores the interests of the child as paramount. The value given to children's interests was embodied in the Children Act (DfES, 2004d) and Every Child Matters (DfES, 2004c) and is expressed in the theme of the 'Unique Child' in the Early Years Foundation Stage (DfES, 2007a). In this, the early years sector has a guiding principle to underpin actions, approaches and decision-making and support managers to lead in a principled manner. Yet, to suggest a single focus on the child oversimplifies the early years context. In the introduction to the Children's Plan (DCSF, 2007), the Secretary of State broadens the focus to 'families': 'more than ever before families will be at the centre of excellent, integrated services that put their needs first, regardless of traditional institutional and professional structures'.

There is no intention to underestimate or over-simplify the task of managing early years settings, nor to suggest that appealing to a strong value base provides easy solutions to complex problems. The proposition is that leading and managing can be supported immensely by reference to the values underpinning early years pedagogy and the commitment to moral purpose which are at the heart of the sector. In Sergiovanni's terms, this creates 'communities of responsibility' which can become self-regulating as, 'not only do members of the community share a common focus, they also feel morally obliged to embody this focus in their behaviour' (2001: 61). The reflection on and review of leadership action and its consequences in relation to that value base can help self-regulation and prompt the search for strategies and principled ways of working.

Exploring the Value/Practice Relationship – Application in Leading and Managing Early Years Settings

Identifying values is not straightforward and, as Smith (2005) suggests, it can be unproductive, if attempted in a pure or abstract fashion. Appealing to absolute values such as truth, justice and freedom produces lists of terms which suggest ideals or result in aspirations for practice which are unachievable, partly because they do not reflect the complexity of life or support solutions to moral dilemmas where values compete. Dahlberg and Moss (2005) view the search for universal codes as dangerous, as they appeal to a technical approach to form judgements based on norms and standards and provide a yardstick for judgement or justification for action which are generally based on rules and rights, producing a legalistic approach and frame of operating. They consider that this 'universalistic ethical approach underlies much policy and practice in the early childhood field' (Dahlberg & Moss, 2005: 67), but warn that such an approach undermines individual responsibility and active engagement with ethical practice.

Roger Smith suggests that we take a broader understanding of values as *'systems of principles and beliefs* which are intended to govern our approach to practice' (Smith 2005: 3). This is more helpful in that it allows scope for multiple perspectives or value positions to be acknowledged and by suggesting these systems are *'intended* to govern', it recognizes that application is not straightforward, that perspectives may sometimes conflict or compete and that a degree of interpretation is required, relative to the situation. If we replaced the term 'govern' with 'guide', then systems of principles and beliefs guiding practice would entail choice and responsibility for decisions in their application. For Dahlberg and Moss (2005), making choices and assuming responsibility are crucial elements of the ethics of care and are fundamental concerns for the early years practitioner in interpreting and fulfilling their responsibilities to others. It recognizes the uncertainty, ambiguity and complexity of the nature of early years practice by promoting active interpretation to make judgements in context, based on guiding principles. It does, however, require openness to scrutiny, reflection and review in order to learn from and improve the process of making professional judgements.

Early years settings are essentially dealing in human relationships in which there are layers and levels of responsibilities to the child, parents and carers, staff, and the wider community. The interface of these relationships can generate uncertainty in how best to fulfil different responsibilities, whether managerial or relating directly to practice, for example, where the needs or interests of the individual compete with the interests of the whole group or where policy directives seem to be at odds with local needs. To enable active interpretation, guiding principles need to be negotiated locally so that sufficient account can be taken of situational factors, the specific context of the setting, the agencies it works with, children and parents and the community it serves because 'it is not possible to develop, say, a localised set of professional principles and ethics in a social and cultural vacuum' (Smith 2005: 3). So, in advocating exploration of values to support principled leadership, we are not seeking a universal code, which could encourage abrogation of responsibility, but a dynamic process of individual and collective analysis of what guides our practice so that we can become more critically aware of the impact of our behaviour and learn from experience.

 Activity

Consider and list what you value in workplace relationships with others:

children   parents   colleagues   staff   manager

Draw out the common words or statements and note them on a card. Place the card in your pocket during your next day at work. At the end of the day or session, take out the card and review where and how you have identified these values in your actions and relationships. What was the response of or the effect on others?

It is proposed that a key leadership function for the early years manager is to allow time and create space and support for themselves and the team to explore individual and collective value positions, principles and beliefs, in order to arrive at a greater understanding of the foundations of their practice and develop their commitment to a common purpose. The intention would be to discover where value positions overlap, agree or disagree, and to negotiate agreed positions where these are essential, while encouraging openness to difference and uncertainty so that operating principles do not become dictates or inhibit development. This is not an easy task and requires the development of an environment which nurtures trusting relationships and values individuals – a theme extended in Chapter 2. Begley (2001) points out that it is also important to achieve a balance between personal, professional, organizational and social values, not necessarily expecting these to be internally consistent but recognizing the legitimacy of all of these in the group, and not allow overriding dominance of one. It is important that this process is not seen as seeking consensus or sameness which could potentially dilute, marginalize or push differences underground. David Clark points out that 'education has a moral quality in that it seeks to discern new values rather than simply adopt or accept uncritically those which already exist' (Clark, 1996: 84). He argues that openness is a core educational value, closely related to inclusivity. This allows for the constructive contesting of practices and beliefs without subjugating the individual to the majority. First, however, it is necessary to build a climate of openness and appreciation of the myriad of influences which contribute to the formulation of our belief systems. Listening and a constructive response is needed to encourage purposeful discussion and a willingness to consider perspectives other than our own.

 Activity

> Take one of the responses to a pause for thought and share it with a trusted colleague. Invite them to do the same.
>
> Once you are comfortable with this, consider taking the activity to a team meeting, after examining what would be needed to prepare the team to enable a 'safe', open and constructive discussion.

Clark (1996) calls for 'an openness to learning as an adventurous and transforming experience' (1996: 8). This requires both the courage and support of others to take risks and venture into new ground based on a belief in a potentially better outcome, ultimately if not immediately. A commitment to the 'moral purpose' of making a positive difference to the lives of children and families can support such risk-taking but only if combined with trust and accountability through self-scrutiny and feedback to inform self-reflection. 'In communities of responsibility it is norms, values, beliefs, purposes, goals, standards, hopes, and dreams that provide the ideas for a morally based leadership' (Sergiovanni, 2001: 62). This type of leadership is self-governing because it is based on shared ideas and does not rely on the authority or personality of positional leadership. Both Fullan (2005) and Sergiovanni (2001) consider that person-dependent leadership does not produce sustainable commitment to learning cultures. Where a team has explored values and purpose together and arrived at a localized set of guiding principles, the leadership is grounded and keeps everyone 'honest'. The positional leader might provide inspiration as a role model in living out the principles in practice and acting with integrity but the shared pedagogy and moral purpose is owned collectively. The role of the positional leader is then more focused on nurturing a culture of learning and capacity to develop and respond to new challenges.

The guiding principles need to be seen as a framework rather than a pre-scription for actions, therefore a system is required for individuals and teams to periodically revisit, reflect, and evaluate provision and practice against their self-determined operating principles and continue the process of revision, adaptation and learning in the light of experience. This relates to the idea of 'double-loop learning' for organizational development, developed by Argyris (1991; Morgan, 1986: 88) where the situation is not simply looked at once to correct errors or as standards of control for accountability, but to enable questioning of operating norms in a more dynamic learning process. A danger of developing statements of operating principles is that they become static and divorced from the reality of everyday practice. Argyris (1991) draws this distinction between what we say and what we do as 'espoused the-ory' and 'theory in use', and he suggests that individuals and groups can learn to identify the inconsistencies, recognize the reasoning behind their actions and change their theories in use. 'Double loop learning requires that we bridge this gulf between theory and reality so that it becomes possible to challenge the values and norms embedded in the theories in use, as well as those that are espoused' (Morgan, 1986: 91). The model of principled leadership proposed in this chapter uses value-based operating principles to guide and review practice. The model bears some resemblance to 'authentic' leadership which Begley (2001: 353) describes as 'a metaphor for professionally effective, ethi-cally sound, and consciously reflective practices in educational admin-istration. This is leadership that is knowledge based, values informed, and skilfully executed.' It provides a perspective for daily as well as strategic actions and interactions.

Point for Reflection

Using the values you have identified in the pauses for thought, consider how, during a day, these values are moulding your leader-ship approach. In the light of these reflections, how can you act to develop your leadership style?

A Framework for Developing Principled Leadership Practice

Principled leadership is not confined to the role of the manager but is potentially present in the whole team. Gill (2006) identifies leadership as both within oneself (intrinsic) and provided by another (extrinsic). 'People who have a vision, know what to do, are self-aware and are self-driven are displaying self-leadership' (Gill, 2006: 11). Sharing moral purpose and pedagogy provides the vision and the knowledge, and exploring the underpinning values and developing operating principles based on them within a team raises self-awareness and drive, thereby encouraging self-leadership within a community of responsibility. Self-awareness is heightened by the reflective review of one's own behaviour and actions in putting the principles into practice, bringing espoused theory and theory in use closer together. Shared reflective review supports collective identification of where and how to close the gap. Settings will therefore need a system for reflection which incorporates the potential for double or repeated loops of learning to support individuals and teams in reviewing the way they work in the interests of children and families.

The EYFS themes for a principled pedagogical approach offer a potential framework which can be placed in a reflective system and applied to the whole work of the setting, including leading and managing in the specific early years context. The EYFS themes can be interpreted beyond the focus on the child to include adults engaged in or associated with the work of the setting. In this way, some operating principles for leading and managing begin to emerge. Thus, the 'Unique Child' becomes the unique person and member of a team, with individual strengths to contribute and the capacity to develop. The individual is valued and seen as competent, capable and resilient. Personal learning and self-knowledge are promoted through reflection and feedback. *Positive relationships* are built on trust and openness, collaboration and support. Deliberate steps are taken by early years managers to create and sustain an ethos and working culture which enables positive relationships to flourish. The working environment is *enabling*, facilitating personal and professional development, providing appropriate challenges with support, encouraging creative thinking and opportunities to try new ways of working. *Learning and development* is recognized as relevant to the whole team and essential for the growth and sustainability of the setting in meeting the needs of the community it serves. A culture of learning is established which recognizes and values individual and professional diversity and is open to different ways of learning.

This application of the themes to principled leadership of the setting can then be placed in a system for reflection based on the EYFS 'Principles into Practice' cards (DfES, 2007a) which offer prompts for reflection formulated into three strands:

- effective practice
- challenges and dilemmas
- reflecting on practice.

Although these cards are designed to support reflection on professional practice in relation to EYFS themes, the three strands are equally suitable for developing a system for reflective leadership practice within early years settings. The system would provide loops of learning by firstly exploring what counts as effective leadership practice in respect of the *unique person, positive working relationships, enabling environment, learning and development.* The next step would be to examine real situations, and to identify the challenges and dilemmas in putting these principles or espoused theory into practice. The third step would be to reflect on the responses to your approach or outcomes of these situations, identifying how you might adapt your approach to further align leadership principles with practice. An essential part of this stage for double-loop learning is to revisit the principles of effective leadership practice to check their validity and appropriateness in different contexts. (An example to demonstrate application is provided in the Personal and Professional Development Activity at the end of the chapter.)

Fullan (2005) advises that in order to build capacity for positive change, we need to develop leadership and this means developing collective abilities, dispositions and motivations through daily interactions, by working harder at working together. 'You need to learn it by doing it and having mechanisms for getting better at it on purpose' (2005: 69).

Summary

The early years sector in Britain is characterized by a market economy and diversity of provision which requires more than regulation and a statutory curriculum to achieve coherence and unity in assuring better outcomes for children and families. Integration of services for a seamless experience for children and families requires a unifying, motivating force which appeals to the sense of 'moral purpose' inherent in the sector. This needs to be coupled with a foundation of guiding principles for the operation of settings, which is negotiated and relevant at local level and suited to the nature of early years. It could be argued that early years pedagogy is underpinned by values and principles which can be translated to provide a system and a reflective framework for developing a principled way of operating, leading and managing early years settings. One approach to developing a framework is to draw on and adapt the EYFS themes and principles into practice cards applicable to leadership and management.

Personal and Professional Development Activity

Applying a reflective framework for principled leadership

A useful starting point would be to:

1   Explore the values underpinning what is understood by *effective practice* in nurturing an *enabling* working environment in your setting.

2   Apply these values consciously to particular leadership and management situations, challenges and dilemmas.

3   Consider what happened and identify:

- where, why and how this contributed to effective practice as currently understood (as in point 1) in order to continue to work in this positive way.

- where, why and how the outcomes or responses were less positive and therefore not contributing to effective practice. This needs to be followed through with the consideration of alternative approaches. What might work better?

- whether the outcome calls into question the assumptions or current understandings of effective practice (as in point 1), prompting a return to review the values and principles which underlie the strategies and practice (double-loop learning).

Suggested Further Reading

Gill, R. (2006) *Theory and Practice of Leadership*. London: Sage.

This is a comprehensive text drawing on various disciplines and studies of leadership in the public and private sector. Gill proposes an integrative, holistic model of leadership.

Smith, R. (2005) *Values and Practice in Children's Services*. Basingstoke: Palgrave Macmillan.

Smith considers value positions and principles central to children's services, demonstrating some value conflicts and suggesting strategies for making considered professional judgements in the best interests of children.

2

Empowering Communities through Inspirational Leadership

Natalie Canning

Chapter Overview

This chapter considers the importance of recognizing the value of individual contributions within an early childhood setting and how these contributions are woven together to support the development and sustainability of a setting. It explores the role of a leader in empowering a setting to be proactive and flexible in its approach to working with children, families and communities and analyses leadership strategies employed within settings to enable inspiring leadership to evolve. The importance of valuing members of staff, the contribution of parents and the relationship between setting, parents and community is examined to reinforce the importance of cultivating a 'valuing culture' within the leadership of settings. Examination of these issues is underpinned by sociological and psychological approaches to the importance of understanding and valuing individuals and being part of a collective team. The aspect of collegiality is a central theme of the chapter, demonstrating the need for a nurturing environment in which an inspirational and empowering leadership style can emerge.

A Small-scale Study

In order to define characteristics to support the role of an inspirational leader, a small-scale study was conducted among a sample of five early years settings. These ranged from a private day nursery to a Children's Centre in the south-west of England. The staff were asked informal, open-ended questions regarding their career journey so far, their perception of the setting and their personal aspirations in terms of working with children. Additionally, respondents were asked about the ethos of the setting, involvement with the immediate community and if they felt valued by their leader or manager. Practitioner voices from the study are provided throughout the chapter to support the emerging concept of inspirational leadership.

Inspiring leadership is a subjective perspective of interactions, intentions, emerging and established relationships and proactive responses to a variety of situations. This chapter analyses key areas of interaction between a community of practitioners and leaders to motivate the setting towards inspirational leadership. It can be challenging to be an inspirational leader without the support of staff, parents and the wider community and this is something that is progressive rather than being achieved by a single action or characteristic. It is a complex web of reflection on actions and reactions to different situations, developing skills to be proactive and responsive to challenges and building relationships which can be sustained. These attributes enable practitioners to be empowered to improve the quality of practice in working with children.

Defining Communities

The leader of a childcare setting not only has the responsibility for the practitioners and children within it, but also the immediate community in which it is situated. In developing relationships with parents, other family members and those professionals who have close associations with the area, the leader's ability to be proactive within the heart of the community is important. Inevitably, this will initially be through interactions with parents, therefore the perception parents have of the setting is important. If a positive association is made, it may lead to supporting, in a small way, a sense of social cohesion with parents working together for the future development of the setting (Martin & Johnson, 1992). To begin to achieve this, the community surrounding the setting requires flexible responses from the leader in order to generate a platform for sharing information, demonstrating a willingness to exchange ideas and inform democratic and collective participation (McClenaghan, 2000).

In real terms and within the context of inspirational leadership, supporting the community is a combination of sharing a common social structure and developing social capital on the basis of forming relationships and gaining mutual trust (Coleman, 1993). This may be a challenge, yet the ability to connect with others is an essential component of an inspirational leader. The collegiality of a setting within a community is reliant on the leader making connections, empowering individuals and providing a flexible transference of informal social learning and development (McClenaghan, 2000). The development of social capital requires the leader to concentrate upon the connections within and between social networks such as those with parents and the local community. In fostering shared interests, tentative steps towards developing trust and collectiveness support the expansion of social capital within the community.

Personal Development – Self-monitoring

A starting point for developing social capital is building personal relationships. This is important in any work context, but particularly when working with children to model an inclusive and welcoming environment. Self-monitoring refers to the way in which practitioners and leaders respond to interactions with others and use the behaviour and reactions of others to guide themselves through the situation rather than trusting their own internal judgment (Gross, 2005). Snyder (1974) introduced the theory of self-monitoring to contribute to the psychology of personality. This theory distinguishes between:

- **high self-monitors**, who monitor and change their behaviour to fit different situations; and

- **low self-monitors**, who are more consistent in their behaviour, think-ing and actions across all types of interactions with other people.

Snyder's theory aligns with trait and situational analysis associated with management and leadership approaches as outlined earlier (Rodd, 2006). It effectively reflects that traits of personality are consis-tent in low self-monitors, whereas a conscious or subconscious change of personality to align with a particular situation is characteristic of high self-monitors. Within the context of analysing inspirational leadership, low and high self-monitoring relates to the way in which leaders approach interrelationships with others. It is important for leaders to become involved in relationships and interactions with oth-ers to build effective communication links and to lead the development and ethos of the setting. The level of awareness an individual may have to the contribution they are making in conversations or group activities will vary depending on their ability to recognize the extent of self-monitoring.

High self-monitors are concerned with responding in a socially appropriate and acceptable manner and are more likely to monitor the situation and look for cues on how to respond, taking the lead from others. They may or may not be aware that they are engaged in this type of behaviour, but they are influenced by other people within the communication exchange. Their behaviour demonstrates situational inconsistency, behaving differently in different situations, reacting to individuals or groups in different ways or demonstrating and expressing behaviour, thoughts or attitudes that conflict with a belief articulated previously (Snyder, 1987). This may be acknowledged as a skill in itself; however, it also demonstrates a lack of trust in the leader's personal internal judgement of how to approach the situation. This does not mean that leaders should treat every situation in the same way, but it does account for a lack of self-assurance to remain true to ideologies and beliefs throughout the exchange. The possible impact of this on others is demonstrated in the following extract from the study.

 Pause for Thought – Practitioner Voice Setting Five

> I used to get really annoyed with my manager – she was so different depending on what situation she was in. One day, I overheard a conversation where she was being really positive about our setting to a new group of parents and really praising the staff. That made me feel really good as a colleague and I had worked really hard in the past couple of weeks implementing a new welcome system for new children. But later in the day she contradicted herself totally and made really negative comments to myself and other staff about the same thing. It is like she is a different person when she is around others and can't give any positives in front of us – it's like she sees it as a sign of weakness.

Leaders who are high self-monitors are skillful in interpreting non-verbal communication and possess perceptiveness and social sensitivity which enables them to interact effectively in diverse situations. But the lack of consistency in dealing with other people will highlight the shallowness of their contribution and over time will become more apparent to those who have close contact with them. A high self-monitor is like a chameleon – changing their colours when they come into contact with others to blend in and be accepted. Leaders are able to function as high self-monitors but they may find it difficult to be inspirational leaders, as they do not tend to demonstrate a true self for fear of rejection or challenge.

Initially, a leader who is a high self-monitor will be quick to establish relationships with staff and will appear to others as being supportive and participative in their leadership. They will demonstrate good listening skills and will provide solutions to short-term challenges. The danger of high self-monitors is that over time, as relationships evolve, a weak foundation will emerge based on a lack of shared understanding or an established value base (as discussed in Chapter 1). Therefore, to be an effective and inspirational leader, a high level of personal functioning is required so that leaders are confident in being able to disclose strengths and recognize their own areas for improvement.

In contrast, low self-monitors are able to remain 'themselves', regardless of the situation and are secure in their beliefs and value base. In situations where low self-monitors find themselves in conflict, they monitor their own behaviour to ensure their values can still be expressed. Initially, this may mean that others find it difficult to adjust to a low self-monitoring leader, especially if they have different values. Leaders who are low self-monitors are able to demonstrate situational consistency, as their behaviour is governed by personal characteristics which are more enduring than the norms associated with different situations. This doesn't mean that a leader is insensitive to others, as they will have a greater awareness of others' needs in any given situation and they are more able to see multiple perspectives. The leader will have a greater sense of self-assurance and be secure in their internal judgment and value base. This is the consistency which is needed in an inspirational leader, to know and be true to oneself whatever the challenge. The low self-monitoring leader is reflective and therefore is able to assess situations, analyse the information being presented, make clear contributions to the progression of the argument and not compromise their own or the setting's position. This is easy to say and may also be easy to recognize but much more difficult to achieve!

How accurately practitioners, parents and the wider community perceive the leadership of an individual is determined partly by their level of self-monitoring and also by how much they reveal about themselves. Self-disclosure is a strategy employed for sharing aspects of personal feelings, values and beliefs with others. By sharing this type of information, leaders and practitioners become more intimate with each other and, as a result, interpersonal relationships are strengthened. Self-disclosure involves risk and vulnerability on the part of the person sharing the information, and therefore it is not simply about providing information to another person but revealing something about their personality, thinking and attitude towards early childhood and leadership.

A high self-monitor may find this challenging, as their sense of self may be subservient because energy is channelled into maintaining a level of false perception to others (James, 1890). Nevertheless, self-disclosure can successfully occur but is more of a calculated response rather than a transparent view of character. A low self-monitor will reveal to a greater extent their sense of self although they will still maintain control over the information they divulge. Self-disclosure occurs on a conscious and subconscious level through what we do and say, as well as what we omit to do and say and therefore over time true characteristics will emerge.

Balancing Self-disclosure

In developing relationships, leaders and practitioners have some control over self-disclosure as it is easier to control verbal behaviour than non-verbal cues. Jourard (1971) believed that the decision to be transparent is a choice and that the aim in disclosing is to be known and to be perceived by others as the person you know yourself to be. Jourard argued that a great deal can be learnt about oneself and others through mutual self-disclosure and, through this, relationship development can be enhanced. Self-disclosure is also a way of maintaining a healthy personality but only if it is an honest portrayal. High self-monitors may find this challenging, especially if the 'picture' that they have been maintaining about themselves is well established. Low self-monitors might be inclined to dominate a situation because they are very comfortable with who they are and so will need to be careful that they do not divulge too much information about themselves, taking the opportunity away from someone else to contribute.

The ability to self-disclose feelings about work-related issues, and the processes involved in developing ideas, rationalizing them and implementing them, make for a very subjective experience. As a leader, to inspire and encourage self-disclosure requires a balance between knowing the fundamental principles and perspectives on which your practice is based and not being selfish in sharing these visions, as they would only become the ethos and vision of the leader and not the whole team. The inspirational leader is careful to support others in expressing their voice without using the process as a cathartic experience.

By building relationships which are based on elements of disclosure, awareness of self-monitoring and a shared interest in the welfare of children, leaders and practitioners will be able to participate in actively building quality relationships within practice as considered in Chapter 5. The inspirational leader needs to keep this agenda at the forefront of any professional development based on self-disclosure, as the point is to develop the thinking and shared interest of the setting, and not for such events to develop into counselling sessions. The skills that are developed as a result of this honest exchange should then be recognized within the context of providing quality provision and not as a set of isolated incidences. This supports practitioners in feeling valued and encourages a willingness to participate in a reciprocal exchange of ideas. Mentoring strategies for providing such support are discussed in Chapter 6.

Nevertheless, getting to the stage of awareness of self-monitoring and having the courage to self-disclose is a daunting task. Inspirational leaders model the thoughts and actions that they would like to develop in their own staff. In early years, one of the biggest challenges that leaders encounter is supporting staff in developing their own self-image.

 Pause for Thought – Practitioner Voice Setting Three

'I want to like my job, but always feel so inferior to my work colleagues. It's not that they say or do anything, it's just the atmosphere and I suppose my own self-doubt.'

Practitioners don't always know why they have a low self-concept but report that they feel 'other practitioners always seem to have more confidence, better qualifications or superior skills' (Practitioner Voice, Setting 3). The idea of even attempting to value oneself in this sort of situation is difficult as vulnerability dominates all thoughts and actions.

 Point for Reflection

- As a leader or manager, how might you react to this?
- What would you do from the point of view of a low self-monitoring inspirational leader?

Developing a Practitioner-centred Culture

Work contexts should support the ideals of a nurturing environment, co-constructed by the leader and staff. Evans (2003) argues that work contexts need to reflect practitioners' ideologies and beliefs. This is something that may be achievable if the values and beliefs of the setting are known and cultivated. Many work environments provide a rhetorical account of what they value and yet the reality for staff may be very different. In talking to staff and observing practice in the five settings, mission statements and value bases seemed to contrast with a lack of direction and generally low morale among the early years teams. The development of self-concept and self-image seemed to be low on the priority list for individuals and leaders and yet they are the most important and influential factors in sustaining a nurturing, productive and happy work context, being shaped by practitioners' perceptions of themselves, not just professionally, but also personally. Through nurturing an environment of self-value, self-esteem and developing self-concept, the teams could be inspired and motivated. But how might this be achieved?

Inspiring leadership builds and supports positive relationships in a work context

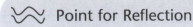

Point for Reflection

Ask yourself:

- How does the leadership in your setting bring out the best in the team?

Initial questions to determine this:

- Does the leadership encourage individual contributions to the development of the setting?
- Does it actively support the sharing of ideas and changes for practice?
- Does it maximize individuals' professional development?
- Does it foster a group unity and reflection on practice?
- Is the work environment compatible with staff needs, expectations, values and ideologies?

By creating work contexts that are conducive to high morale, job satisfaction and motivation, positive job-related attitudes are developed. However, in many cases, settings do not provide an environment conducive to supporting this type of development. This is somewhat of a paradox when considering the ethos, principles and perspectives in early childhood. The Early Years Foundation Stage (EYFS) (DfES, 2007a) principles – and especially the themes that focus upon building positive relationships and enabling environments – are significant to developing a fluid transference of knowledge and understanding in linking inspirational leadership and working with children.

Good practice reflects a 'child-centred' approach, meeting individual needs in order to develop well-being, belonging, contribution, communication and exploration (Pound, 2005). A 'practitioner-centred' approach considers care, solicitude and an interest in co-workers' welfare which supports a unified approach to working with others (Evans, 2003). Practitioners acknowledge that children have an abundance of skills, abilities and competences but these are also the skills that should be acknowledged in practitioners by leaders and others within a setting.

A child-centred approach was expressed as being a key feature in the settings involved in the study, when identifying qualities of inspirational leadership. All agreed that supporting children to develop holistically was a core belief and that children's emotional and social well-being was crucial. When asked whether they thought the approach by their leader adopted similar qualities in working with staff, there was a mixed response.

Pause for Thought – Practitioner Voice Setting One

'We believe in offering a child-centred experience to children and that is evident in the work we do with the children, but it is a different matter for the staff. There is definitely not a practitioner-centred ethos! I don't think you would ever be able to persuade our manager that you could achieve both.'

'We have elements of a practitioner-centred working environment, but only when it suits. In a way, that is harder to deal with as we never know where we stand. When I first came here, I thought it was very much child- and practitioner-centred but I soon realized I was only given the support because I was new.'

To demonstrate the correlation between child-centred and practitioner-centred work, an ethos which supports the approach of interweaving values and beliefs into a work context should be adopted. In New Zealand, Te Whariki is such a philosophy which states that an underlying principle in working with children is to 'give respect for children and their learning which seeks to identify and value diversity' (Pound, 2005: 69). Te Whariki is a framework providing for children's early learning and development within a social and cultural context which emphasizes the learning partnership between practitioners, parents and families. Its principles are based on a holistic curriculum in response to children's learning and development in the setting and the wider context of the child's world.

For a leader to establish a practitioner-centred environment, the same principles should be upheld. If practitioners are to develop their own skills in providing a nurturing environment for children to develop holistically, then their own experiences within that environment also have to be nurturing and positive. In developing inspirational leadership, the underlying principles and perspectives for working with children need to be mirrored in supporting staff. To begin to achieve this, the leader needs to firstly consider individual staff needs and perspectives, before attempting to bring values and beliefs together to form a collective ethos (Evans, 2003).

Within the study for this chapter, practitioners confirmed that they felt most contented in their roles when respected for the skills they possessed, empowered and trusted to carry out their responsibilities and where they had built positive relationships with their co-workers and leader. One suggested that inspirational leadership was when 'the setting works in harmony to provide the very best opportunities for children and staff to develop' (Setting 2). This supports the underpinning values of Te Whariki where attention is paid to the context and people involved in the setting and where there is an enabling environment for the strengths of practitioners and children to be developed further.

Value Bonds in Enabling Environments

To support early years settings to develop an enabling environment, the formulation of a 'bond of values' may be a way of developing an ethos which is inclusive of individual needs, group beliefs and leadership ideals. Staff should be empowered to make direct links with their needs and the setting's qualities, in order to co-construct a set of values that have real meaning to all within the team. The 'bond' will be an open and fluid document that is subject to ongoing development and modification through continuous reflective practice. Inspirational leadership will then have an opportunity to facilitate a positive and forward-thinking culture within the setting and among the team.

What becomes apparent in the formulation of a bond of values, are not only individual perspectives but also the extent of knowledge and understanding about working with children. The process highlights any gaps in knowledge and sometimes the more controversial views individuals hold. As a tool for empowering staff and reinforcing the group, a value bond can be a positive experience if not contentious and challenging for all involved!

 Pause for Thought – Practitioner Voice Setting Two

'In our setting, we thought forming a value bond would be a simple yet effective continuous professional development activity as we were quite a close team and knew each other's practice well. When we sat down to write about our values on play, we ended up having quite heated discussions! I learnt more about the people I worked with and where they were coming from in doing this than I had in the past year and a half of working with them! Looking back, the experience was really challenging and it took ages, but now I feel like the setting has a purposeful direction.'

A value bond should be viewed as a long-term development goal for a setting. It will take a long time to agree and may never be fully accepted by everyone. It should stay as 'work in progress' to continually challenge the team so that they do not get complacent. The outcome of the bond is not as important as the process that each individual goes through in developing understanding of their professional values and of each other. The inspirational leader needs to play a facilitative role in valuing every contribution and negotiating with the team on contentious issues.

Process-led activities and development are essential for inspirational leadership. They are the most difficult to conduct, but essential to the personal and professional growth of staff. Ringer (2002: 27) argues that 'people in a team often act as if something is true, even when the majority of team members know it is not'. The ability to empower individuals to find their own 'voice' is a difficult task. In many settings, there will be challenges faced when encouraging practitioners to be open with others, to feel 'safe' in expressing their views and opinions in a peer environment or to have the confidence to fully participate. To address these issues, it is essential to return to good practice in working with children.

〰 Point for Reflection

In answering these questions on how you empower children, apply the same principles to working towards empowering and inspiring staff:

- How do I support children's/adults' self-esteem?
- How do I encourage communication in the team?
- Am I aware of the verbal and non-verbal communication displayed when working with children/adults? What principles do I follow?
- How do I support adults in transitions and developing relationships?
- How do I empathize with children when they are feeling vulnerable in my setting?
- Why is this important?

The process of empowering staff involves the setting moving towards a 'learning organization' (Leithwood & Aitken, 1995) where there is a collective commitment to common purposes and values. As a group, practitioners are then able to modify and continually develop more effective ways of accomplishing those purposes which are meaningful to the individual and the whole. By exploring individual beliefs and ideologies about early childhood in the working day, the foundation of self-concept is developed, the value base for the setting is established and a sense of belonging is fostered in the team.

The challenge is to enable an environment in which individual and collective learning can be channelled and values built into the conditions of the setting. This may be achieved through enabling opportunities within the setting that allow frequent interaction and authentic participation in key decisions.

 Pause for Thought – Practitioner Voice Setting Three

'When our setting was going through the process of changing into a children's centre, our manager involved all of the staff so that we felt part of the move, rather than it being just something that we had no control over. We went through a period of consultation where we could put our ideas forward for different working practices and some of them were introduced. The main thing was that we were involved, and even though it was always going to happen, it didn't feel as if we didn't matter.'

Inspirational leadership is being able to juggle all of the variables, meet the needs of practitioners, parents, the wider community and external agencies while being pulled in different directions. An inspirational leader negotiates the tensions and ambiguities, for example, buffering staff from external pressures that may conflict with the setting's ethos but also ensuring that they know about influences which will have an impact on practice, such as the move from a nursery to a Children's Centre.

Inspirational leadership is also about having a strategic overview to establish a framework for process development. This requires openness in communication exchanges and a clear vision of conceptual coherence to support the growth of the setting's culture towards collegiality.

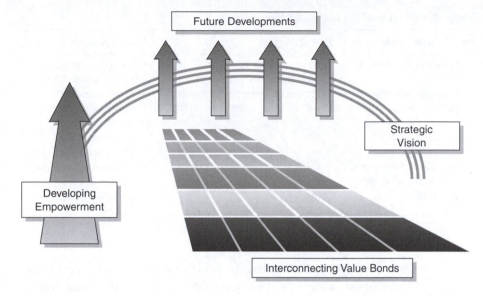

Figure 2.1   Enabling development of value bonds

Developing Hot Qualities

In developing a coherent vision for a setting, the elements of relationship development, communication, practitioner value systems and the fostering of both a child- and practitioner-centred approach require a range of leadership skills. These elements all feed into the cultural basis for the setting and establish the extent to which the team will become involved with, and influence, the immediate community. Hot management is an approach to leadership which analyses how a leader is able to foster a proactive and visionary culture within a setting (Bottery, 2003). This approach initially requires a 'safe' peer environment, developing a culture of openness and an ability to discuss daily issues within the setting and wider community. In supporting an environment that is inclusive of different perspectives and sensitive to others' values, hot management is an effective and efficient way in which to capture the mind, motivate and gain commitment of not only an individual but of the collective staff (Bottery, 2003).

To begin with, hot management establishes the basic assumptions which are evident within every setting and immediate community (Schein, 1985). These could be the routines of the setting, approaches to healthy eating, communications with parents or involvement in community activities, for example. The leader then groups the assumptions, in

Table 2.1   Hot qualities for leadership

Hot Management	Hot Qualities	Hot Practice
• Openness within the setting • Inclusion of different perspectives	• Motivation and commitment to the setting within staff • Process-driven development, not outcome-led	• Evident shared ethos/value base • Opportunities for reflection on personal and professional development
• Establishment of basic assumptions within the setting	• Give-and-take relationship between practitioners and leaders	• Proactivity in regard to early years provision and practice

collaboration with staff, according to whether they have been consciously developed to improve practice or have unconsciously evolved in the day-to-day routine of the setting. The most important aspect of this process is to decide to what extent these assumptions have become embedded as part of the ethos, result from external pressures or are the consequence of internal bureaucracy. This approach involves a level of scrutiny in every aspect of practice. This is why a vital element of this activity is for the leader to have already established positive relationships with all staff, so that the exercise does not turn into creating a blame culture or perpetuating feelings of anxiety.

An indication of the success of such an activity is when staff are self-motivated, working for the advancement of the setting and their own professional development. This is where 'hot' qualities are developed and start to become embedded in the fabric of the setting. The inspirational leader fosters a desire in staff to know their internal values in relation to their practice. There should be evidence of a balance between practitioners' individual willingness to contribute to the progression of the setting and an inspirational leader to confirm and maintain those values. These characteristics displayed by leaders and practitioners in order to achieve this become 'hot' qualities within the team, demonstrating a movement from compliance to commitment. It supports a 'give and take' relationship, leading to a process-driven culture rather than outcome-led management.

To foster the value of organizational commitment, the strategy of identifying 'hot' qualities in teams means that the relationships developed between parents and the immediate community are equally as important

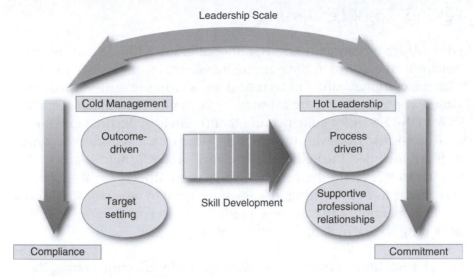

Figure 2.2 Hot qualities within teams

as fostering the relationships in staff. An inspirational leader will not only meet the parents' needs for their children but will encourage a change of attitude towards a positive disposition of sharing information and skills (this is discussed further in Chapter 7). A sense of ownership for staff and parents can empower individuals to contribute to the support mechanisms involved in creating, building and maintaining internal value systems and therefore result in 'hot' practice. This process should not be deterministic, but support a flexible structure allowing for reflection on the part of the inspirational leader and practitioners. The following extract demonstrates how this is not only important for the development of the setting but also for individuals.

 Pause for Thought – Practitioner Voice Setting Four

'It is great to see people who would not normally come into [the setting]. The stay and play group has been really successful, I think, because we don't put any pressure on the parents or extended family members to contribute. The group has slowly gained in popularity and now it's not just an opportunity to spend a little quality time with their children, but also to socialize and be part of the community. I can really see how this contributes to the development of the community and the great thing is that people now know who I am outside of work so I feel I am building my own positive relationships.'

Letting Go of Leadership

For a leader to maintain an inspirational ethos within a setting, they must find the key to 'interconnectedness'. This is the ability to recognize the complex nature of relationships within the setting while providing a level of psychological stability (Schaffer, 1996). Staff members look to the leader for guidance and to ultimately make final judgments and decisions. However, in moving towards an environment where staff are included in the decision-making process, there is a need for mutual trust. Practitioners need to value each other's perspectives and contributions to the setting, relationships need to be established and a level of openness and tolerance needs to be accepted before staff will be willing to risk making changes to their practice.

For a leader, the ultimate trust is 'letting go' of staff, empowering them to grow as practitioners and to support them in gaining ownership of their roles and responsibilities. However, this doesn't just happen. Whatever the level of relationship between leader and staff in a setting, the ability to 'let go' requires careful foundations to be laid. Within a setting, a collective ethos for valuing individuals should be established.

In traditional leadership environments, the 'power' sits with the leader's ideas and beliefs (a transactional approach). The leader's objectives filter through the establishment to reflect and shape the management of the setting (a top–down approach). In letting go of leadership, the power is disseminated among the staff, supporting their empowerment and enabling possibilities for change and development. The focus for the team changes therefore from 'what can be done' within the constraints of time, resources and willingness of staff to 'what really makes a difference' for the setting (Levin, 2003). A 'letting go' approach is similar in value base to transformational leadership or participatory management, in that a confidence in practitioners' ability to provide quality practice supports individual autonomy and an interchange of ideas and developments for the setting (Rodd, 2006). However, this approach requires a high element of trust and respect from a team, centred on the same vision and value base for the setting as there is a mutual dependency between staff and leadership.

Without practitioners, leadership cannot function and without leadership, practitioners may have no coherent vision or direction. If the scales are tipped one way or the other, there will be a disparity between the responsibilities of either role, leading to discontent for all involved. Inspiring leadership is about striking a balance to develop a vision for the setting but distributing power to the staff so that they have involvement in the evolution of the setting.

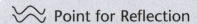 **Point for Reflection**

How have you established a culture of 'trust' in your setting?

If there is limited trust in your setting, then consider why that might be the case.

- What mechanisms have you got in place that foster an environment of trust between practitioners?
- Which 'hot qualities' are evident in the setting to support relationships between staff and leadership?
- Which aspects of the setting provide an inclusive environment where there is potential to 'let go' of leadership?

Summary – Inspired to Be Inspiring?

This chapter has considered ways in which the leader can support staff to develop quality relationships and generate a solid foundation of knowledge and skills in working with children. The leader cannot be inspirational if there is no one to be inspirational for and practitioners have a key role in the development of ethos and vision. The shared values that are moulded through this process are significant in creating an inclusive and nurturing environment, not just for practitioners but also for children and their families.

Being an inspirational leader is about having an awareness of the complex strands that individuals bring to a workplace and of how to weave these together to provide strong foundations for the development of the setting. An investment in time to consider the impact of change and development on staff and the immediate community is vital and the ability to recognize personal strengths and vulnerability is also important. Being inspiring in leadership is not about being invincible. Support is needed from staff to build trust and shared thinking so that the setting becomes empowered and is inspirational for the wider community.

Personal and Professional Development Activity

Identify in your practice elements of inspirational leadership which relate to the ideas presented within this chapter.

Consider working on one of the following activities to support collegiality within your setting:

- Develop a Value Bond based on an aspect of your practice.

- Re-consider your setting's ethos to reflect a 'practitioner-centred' approach as well as a 'child-centred' approach.

- Reflect on the 'hot qualities' in your own practice and within your setting.

Can you identify in your own practice examples of high and low self-monitoring? What type of support systems could you implement to develop practitioners' understanding and awareness of this personal development?

Suggested Further Reading

Johnson, S. (1998) *Who Moved My Cheese?* London: Vermilion.

This book considers different attitudes towards change and how it may be effectively managed, and supports personal reflection in assessing the ability to respond to change.

Rodd, J. (2006) *Leadership in Early Childhood* (3rd edn). Buckingham: OUP.

Chapter 8 of Rodd's book considers building and leading teams, discussing the practicalities of achieving quality leadership within team development.

Snyder, M. (1974) 'Self-monitoring of Expressive Behaviour.' *Journal of Personality and Social Psychology.* 30(4): 526–37.

Snyder designed a questionnaire to assess self-monitoring called the Self-Monitoring Scale. It consisted of 25 questions measuring an individual's concern of impressions made to other people and an ability to control the impressions that they conveyed to others in social situations.

3

Managing Change and Pedagogical Leadership

Mandy Andrews

Chapter Overview

This chapter explores the nature of change in early childhood settings. It acknowledges that many early childhood leaders confess to a lack of skills in change management and explores how they can draw upon their understanding of pedagogical practices to inform leadership skills and the development of a 'change embracing' organization. Pictures of Practice illustrate the links between pedagogic practices with children and pedagogy-based leadership of adults. The chapter concludes with a consideration of the need to establish and sustain early childhood organizations as emotionally safe spaces for staff in order to facilitate safe spaces for children's development.

Why Do We Need to Know how to Manage Change in the Early Years?

Early childhood services, and the staff working within them, are currently at the receiving end of an unprecedented amount of public interest, public policy, legislation and related guidance. Some early childhood settings are facing challenges of expansion (of numbers, hours of opening, early education provision), while others are facing changes enforced by restricted and reducing budgets as a result of policy change, population flexibility, and new structures. Each setting will have a different set of specific change issues as a result.

Change is often promoted as a positive activity and one to be embraced in our post-modernist society in which 'uncertainty is our only certainty' (Dahlberg et al.,1999: 186). Jillian Rodd argues that change is a 'natural phenomenon in all aspects of our lives' (Rodd, 2006: 181). Charles Handy goes further in considering that change is one of the inevitable paradoxes of life, a life which he demonstrates as a series of sigmoid curves reflecting the way that things grow, wax and wane. To picture this, imagine a series of rising waves, each higher than the last.

Handy's (1994) sigmoid curve is therefore a change curve that drops before rising to the top of an arc, and then falling again like the lee of a wave. He indicates that leaders need to be aware of this flux and either change to start a new sigmoid curve before the top of the upward arc, or else risk the threat of failure as the organization begins to stagnate once it has passed over the crest of the wave: 'wise are they who start the second curve ... to build a new future while maintaining the present' (Handy, 1994: 50).

We only need to consider how there is re-growth after a fire, or a receding flood, to understand that change not only challenges, but also refreshes and stimulates, new growth or adaptation. Fullan argues that change is essential for continual improvement: '... when things are unsettled, we can find new ways to move ahead and create breakthroughs that are not possible in stagnant societies' (Fullan, 2004: 1). Those who have had experience of establishing new early childhood settings, such as Children's Centres, will perhaps be aware of this implementation curve and how early anxieties are subsequently replaced by a surge forward with new initiatives and the energy of development; only to be followed later by the concerns of consolidation and sustainability.

This chapter considers the management of change and it may be helpful at this point to continue with the watery metaphor and consider the organization as a ship with the leader as captain. A charismatic captain riding at the front of the ship will concentrate on forging ahead, and present an exciting figure riding each crest of the wave. Successful captains will be ready for the next wave. They shout 'come with me' and the team follows, with adventurous enthusiasm. To outside observers, they may seem vibrant and exciting adventurers. However, if we were to follow that ship for a period of time, and look more closely we may find that the leader is looking forward so keenly that the maintenance of the boat is neglected, and the rear of the boat (the staff team and engine) is merely trailing along behind in trust. The charismatic captain is aware of his or her own image, and will move on when the energy of the team begins to wane, but forgets to look behind. When the charismatic captain is gone, the 'engine' will not have the instruction or independent capacity to function and it will be at the mercy of fate, awaiting a new charismatic leader. Contrast this bleak metaphorical image with one of a magnanimous captain who takes care of his or her maintenance duties and staff team, who manages from the middle of the ship, and who supports the rising abilities of the staff team, perhaps with all team members looking out for the future. In distributing leadership roles, the leader makes time to consider, plan and prepare for future challenges. In such a ship, the team will develop the ability to maintain and support its own integrity.

The environment in which early childhood settings operate may seem like an unpredictable sea at times. Leaders may be facing stormy seas of new change led by external forces, perhaps national politics. Children's Centre leaders may have to accept and respond to external change influences, and adapt to meet the new demands of the latest guidance, model or legislation. Perhaps the seas of change are less rough and unpredictable arising from quality concerns, new interests and understandings about best practice, and responding to financial incentives for growth. Setting leaders are often deeply passionate about subtle continual improvements to their practice, in response to their moral desire to offer the best opportunity possible for the children they support. There are therefore two ends of the change spectrum – the one end being change in response to external stimuli and the other a calmer internally motivated change for quality improvement.

In the current political and social climate, the ability to lead change is expected as 'change is a recurrent theme in the life of education in the UK' (Moore, 2007: 1). It is promoted as being beneficial to learning and transforming organizations (Carnall, 1991; Harris & Lambert, 2003; Fullan, 2004), and it is becoming accepted that strong leadership requires evidence of the ability to stimulate and manage change and to support adaptation in others (Handy, 1994; Harris & Lambert, 2003; Fullan, 2004). However, Jillian Rodd (2006) points to research demonstrating that many early childhood professionals do not have a clear concept of several aspects of leadership, among which were change management abilities. Early childhood professionals do, on the other hand, have experience and a theoretical understanding of how to support children's changing processes of learning and development – their pedagogic practices. These pedagogic understandings which support developmental change in children can be used to inform leadership and approaches to managing change.

The Varying Nature of Change in Early Childhood Settings

Both Handy and Rodd inform us that organizations are dynamic entities, and early childhood organizations are no different since there are many types of change which may be experienced in the annual cycle. Rodd identifies six key types of change:

- **Incremental** – small day-to-day modifications.

- **Induced** – a conscious decision to implement a change in people, processes, programmes, structures and systems.

- **Routine** – effected by the leaders on a daily basis in response to problem situations with the aim of restoring the status quo.

- **Crisis** – in response to an unexpected occurrence within the setting.

- **Innovative** – resulting from creative problem-solving or trial and error, in which the team leader and members are seeking more successful ways to further the mission and meet objectives.

- **Transformational** – where the form of an organization is radically altered, such change occurring at a crisis point when the survival of the organization calls for drastic action. Rodd sees the creation of the new multidisciplinary Children's Centres and childcare in primary schools as an example of transformational change (Rodd, 2006: 186).

Rodd feels that change occurs in a variety of ways and involves different levels of significance for those affected (Rodd, 2006). It is perhaps the site of the power base driving the change that affects its impact upon the staff team and the quality of the children's environment. In the change models indicated above, it is clear that there are some changes which are owned by the organization, its staff and community, which form part of the internal dynamics of those organizations continually striving for improvement – Rodd's 'innovative' model is of this type. Other types of change can be externally imposed as a result of politics, reduced funding, falling income, new

Table 3.1 Participation, power and change

Arnstein's 8 'rungs'	Change Leadership Models
Manipulation Therapy Informing	Quick fix
Consultation Placation	Reactive
Partnership	Planned and programmed change
Delegated power	Tweaking and testing
Citizen (practitioner) control	Expediency

legislation, or local authority planned strategic initiatives. In these cases, the staff, and indeed the leader, may feel quite disempowered by the change process, feeling it is out of their control. Yet other changes may be internally initiated but still imposed, perhaps by a new charismatic leader, or an insecure manager who wishes to establish a power base. While this may assert the authority of the new leader, it may also cause problems as staff lose that sense of personal responsibility and ownership of their area of work. Aspects of these interpersonal dynamics are further explored in Chapters 2 and 3.

Arnstein (1969) considered issues of citizen participation in society and identified eight 'rungs' of empowerment, from manipulation to citizen control. In Table 3.1, Arnstein's eight 'rungs' are adapted and compared to potential change models to illustrate team empowerment issues. These are presented in a reversed hierarchical order from autocratic leadership through staff participation, to staff control.

A 'quick fix' change, as outlined at the top of the right-hand column, will very often be that type of change implemented initially by one person in a top–down fashion. At the bottom of the ladder are those types of change which clearly relate to practitioner control, and may even shift the power base onto the practitioner in their own domain, and undermine the leader. Models close to the centre will be those which will recognize the need for a level of responsibility to reside in the leader, but which also recognize that information and solutions may reside in different areas of the team.

- **A quick fix** – a speedy, often structural change, implemented from the top, for an externally visible effect. Closing a setting after a poor Ofsted inspection may be an example of such highly visible quick fix change, in which power resides with the implementer. Emergency procedures often require such speedy authoritarian responses (consider how a fire drill is operated) as they are efficient. Staff have little ownership of the process and 'do as they are told'.

- **Reactive change** – close to quick fix, this requires a change in response to something that has given a 'cognitive jar' (Piaget, 1977) to the organization and its staff team, but which involves some team and community members in devising the solution. This may be largely approached through team consultation, or the more empowering informed partnership. Reactive change involves a more considered formulation of a response to an externally perceived failing or shortfall than the 'quick fix'. It may be used to perhaps address a recommendation in an Ofsted report, or the need for staff training and discussion around implementation of a new legal and practice requirement such as the Early Years Foundation Stage (EYFS) (DfES, 2007a).

- **Planned and programmed change for organizational improvement** – this offers a more constructive approach, responding to the external environment and working to further develop the positives of the existing internal environment. Perhaps the team take time to look at one area of practice at each staff meeting, and consider strengths and areas for improvement. Suggestions are received from 'the team' and possibly some research is undertaken. The expectation is that resulting changes will be 'owned' by all and implemented within a fixed timeframe, but one that is locally reasoned and justified. There is usually a large body of commitment to the changes suggested through such team process, even though one or a few people may be delegated the authority to carry the project forward.

- **Tweaking and testing change** – consistent with Claxton's (1997) 'Slow Knowing', this is a change model presented by Fullan (2004) in which time is taken by leaders and teams to 'soak up' experiences of complex domains, and to seek to realize the subtle patterns and qualitative understandings within them. In this model, front-line staff, with close understanding of the issues, are recognized as having detailed practice knowledge and are encouraged to continually make small changes and innovations as required to improve quality and outcomes. This approach involves a gradual process of reviewing and modifying in action, tweaking something, examining the results, reflecting and learning and perhaps tweaking a little more. Sometimes this revisiting will result in giving up that idea, service or process, for a movement in another direction. Changes implemented in this way are subtle and ongoing. They may be deeply embedded in the culture of the staff team. An example of this tweaking and testing change may be a voluntary sector community project, run by local parents, which has been running for decades and has established and maintained its own particular culture and value base – evolving over a period of time to implement a particular way of working to meet local needs.

- **Expediency** – these are the day-to-day changes implemented by a team in response to daily challenges, or personal needs. There are probably many such changes occurring in most organizations, and many will be adopted in the spirit of teamwork and best endeavour. However, in this model such changes may be implemented with an eye on expediency by and for staff. Depending on the stimulus, such changes can go unnoticed for some time by an uninvolved leader, and may result in an organization or department shift in an unwanted direction. The power base for such change is clearly held by the front-line practitioner, who may make the changes covertly, without necessarily consulting others or considering the bigger picture and key outcome intentions.

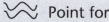 Point for Reflection

Rodd (2006) found that early childhood leaders often focused on maintenance, rather than change for improvement.

- What is your perception of change in your setting?
- Where does the focus and power of change reside with regard to your setting?
- Where on the ladder of participation do your experiences of change sit?

What Impacts Can Change Have on the Organizational 'Team', Families and Children?

Recent unpublished research by the author has identified that organizational structural change does have an impact on a practitioner's focus on child and family outcomes. One member of staff interviewed clearly stated this: 'I feel that the focus on the children and families has dropped during this change process; there is a lack of motivation among staff' (Andrews, 2007). Friedman (2005) argues that structural change is rarely a good thing as 'reorganizations take two years out of the life of any organization while people try to figure out their new jobs and how they fit into any new arrangement' (2005: 33). He also considers that 'there is almost nothing that needs to be done that cannot be done with the existing organization if there is the will to do it' (2005: 33). For Friedman, it is the desired outcome that is important, not a demonstrable ability to change.

Anton Obholzer also queries the purpose of any proposed changes: 'will the changes serve the primary task or not?' (Obholzer & Zagier Roberts, 1994: 207). He recognizes that practitioners often exhibit resistance to change and further asks: 'is the resistance to change ... a movement to safeguard the task against changes which are actually in themselves anti-task?' In other words, does the staff team consider that the new initiatives are destructive and opposed to their own awareness of the current outcomes they have already signed up to? Have the setting's values changed without the staff team being aware of the extent of the changes? Different practitioners will perhaps have slightly different views on the primary task of a setting and may need further explanation of the reasons behind changes for them to accept a new task or adapted approach – explored in relation to Chapter 7.

 Point for Reflection

Is the practitioner's perception of the change process and ownership of the change process important to you?

How can you promote ownership of change initiatives in your setting?

Change Embracing, Holding and Containing Organizations

Contemporary early childhood leaders need to draw upon and adapt their key professional principles to enable them to adopt, with integrity, change leadership responses appropriate for their current context. Table 3.2 demonstrates the four themes of the EYFS (DfES, 2007a) interpreted in relation to leadership.

Table 3.2 The four themes of the EYFS translated to inform leadership

1. People are competent learners from birth who can be resilient, capable, confident and assured.
2. People learn to be strong and independent from a base of secure relationships with others.
3. The environment plays a key role in supporting people's development and learning.
4. People develop and learn in different ways and at different rates, and different types of learning and development may be equally important and interconnected.

Using the example of the third theme we know that children need safe, stimulating environments in which there are patterns such as flexible routines and an element of consistency in layout. Such predictability provides a level of security from which a child can explore. Are needs so very different for the adults working and learning in the organizations which exist to support children's development? Jon Stokes acknowledges that traditional, perhaps unchanging, organizations have historically provided staff with a sense of continuity and stability which 'held' and 'contained' anxieties as a result (Stokes, 1994: 125). He goes on to say that today's rapidly changing organizations create an increase in interpersonal stress and tension.

It is widely recognized that such emotional strains are common patterns of response to change (Kubler-Ross, 1969; Carnall, 1991; Fullan, 2004). Traditionally, change could be seen as a 'project' which is implemented over a period of time, and which appears to be implemented from above. In reality today, there may be many change curves operating at the same time within an organization. Each may have a similar pattern of initial anxiety and denial, replaced gradually by despair, then acceptance over the period of implementation as people experience the positive impact of the new change, or draw on an accepting resilience.

Picture of Practice

Quick Fix and Dialogue Repair

In 2005, Children's Centres received guidance that a teacher should be recruited to model good practice to existing early childhood practitioners in the Children's Centre nurseries. This new role imposed in a top–down

(Continued)

(Continued)

fashion in the nursery, in response to this external stimulus, was perceived as a threat to the existing nursery nurse's professionalism and work boundaries. In time, and with frank discussion and acknowledgement of feelings, both parties recognized their different strengths. The nursery nurses realized that their fears had been emotive responses and that they had learnt from the teacher's different approach. The teacher recognized the wealth of skill and close knowledge of the children that existed in the nursery nurses and also adapted. With hindsight, the leader realized that she should have taken time to consult with the nursery staff in implementing the imposed change – to identify with them the skills they needed support with and to give them the opportunity to participate in the change process in an empowered way.

There is, as we have identified, a great deal of potential resistance to change. A change in routine can lead to emotional responses such as disorientation. If the purpose of the change has not been clearly identified there may be confusion, with the team 'not quite getting things right'. The staff team may initially deny that any change will happen: 'it will not affect us', 'we have always done it this way so we will be OK'. They may defend their existing practices and approaches: 'why should it change, as we are doing OK?', 'we won't let them change things'. Gradually, it becomes evident that the change is inevitable for a variety of reasons: 'well, we might as well get on with it'. The team may, at different rates, begin to discard their existing ways of working and adapt to new ways.

In the early period of denial and defence, practitioners may show anger and frustration at feeling 'out of control'. Gradually, the anger subsides, the team recovers and re-establishes a level of self-esteem and respect. Performance will perhaps be higher, and things will continue, with the new changes incorporated (until the next change process begins).

Fullan writes of a similar change process in his 'implementation dip' (Fullan 2004: 75). For him, the implementation dip is experienced in both lowered performance and confidence as people become engaged in a task that needs new skills and understanding. He writes that innovations call on people to change their behaviours, or perhaps their beliefs. People who were previously confident in what they were doing can often feel anxious, fearful, confused, overwhelmed, de-skilled or even disturbed. Fullan argues that ineffective leaders (consider our charismatic captain) have no empathy for people undergoing implementation dips (2004: 51). Effective early child-hood leaders on the other hand can draw on their pedagogic under-standings and recognize that staff faced with imposed change are experiencing both the social/physiological fear of change, and the lack of technical know-how to make the change work quickly. As early childhood practitioners, effective change leaders should sup-port both the emotional well-being and skills development of staff. Mujis et al. (2004) cite research which highlights the fact that teach-ers want their managers to listen to them, to provide for the physi-cal, emotional and social needs of the organization, to give them trust, time, tools and the support needed to succeed, and to have a vision which they can share. It could be expected that these same needs exist in early childhood teams.

> ### 〰 Point for Reflection
>
> If someone else is telling you what to do, you probably feel that your 'humanness' is restricted. Toddlers have tantrums as their uniqueness and understanding of self-determination grows in them and they have a greater sense of restrictions placed upon them by adults, or their lack of skill and ability. Adults similarly have periods of frustration when they are unable to have a sense of self-determination and autonomy.
>
> Could the change process for my team be eased if I can find a way of addressing the emotional and skills needs of my practitioner team?

Consider now Piaget's concept of disequilibriation and its 'affect' responses (Piaget, 1977). Drawing on pedagogic theory again, we can gain understanding to help new leaders support common reactions to change. For Piaget, disequilibriation happens when expectations, based on past and current knowledge, are not confirmed. For some reason, there is a difference between reality and the expectation of an experience. This lack of a 'match' causes a primitive emotional response of anger or frustration and original positions and beliefs are defended against this attack. This explains the 'implementation dip' and change curve responses. In children, this may be evidenced in cries of frustration or outbursts of anger as they cannot achieve what they expected to do. Early childhood practitioners may recognize such anger and help to support the child through the learning curve, as time is taken to recognize the feelings, support them and 'scaffold' alternative responses or new ways of working (Bruner, 1990).

Children and the adults that work with them need a secure environment in which to embrace change, explore, adapt and develop

Staff need to know that their emotions will be looked after and that they will be given time to visit and revisit new tasks and actions in order to become skilled practitioners, operating at a new level of understanding and development. Strategies to assist this process can be found in the pedagogic theories of Donald Winnicott and Wilfred Bion. Winnicott (1971) argues that mothers are able to 'hold their babies in mind', and in so doing provide a base of security from which the child can confidently explore. Bion (1962) argues that parents and carers of young children are able to 'contain' emotional stress by recognizing the stress and transmitting back to the child a sense of acknowledgement and reassurance with understanding. For example, a child that is anxious because they have just hurt themselves can be reassured when they are crying as someone steps in to support their emotions: 'I know, it hurts'... and explains what has happened and that they will survive this moment: 'you have had a nasty bump, and it's sore ... but it will stop bleeding soon'.

In a similar vein, Obholzer and Zagier Roberts (1994) recognize that there is a human need for an organization, including work organizations, to be a 'container' for adults' social and emotional anxieties. Stokes (1994) illuminates how, with the increasing recognition of plurality in our society, existing structures which traditionally formed these anxiety 'containers' are being challenged – creating considerable additional stress and confusion for the members of the organization, and of society. The 'holding' of anxieties breaks down. He argues that, as a result, conflicts between sub-groups are forced down to the inter-personal level with a notable increase in bullying and other forms of 'scapegoating' (Stokes, 1994: 125).

Where babies are not supported with a secure base, they are less inclined to be self-reliant and exploratory (Winnicott, 1971). The same appears to be true for adults. Where there is insecurity and stress for practitioners, there is often less innovation to be seen since it may be stifled by the fear of correction and a greater sense of risk. Those who do nothing unusual will be less noticed and so a 'non-innovative' neutral and stagnant culture could be created. Where there is less innovation in the workforce, there must be more direc-tion from the top, which can lead to a spiral of increased challenge, greater loss of autonomy and further frustration.

How Else Might Pedagogical Principles Help Strong Leadership and Appropriate Management of Change?

Mujis et al. (2004) identified that directors of early childhood set-tings felt less prepared to deal with staffing issues and workload, and best prepared for teaching children. There is, in Children's Centres, an increasing awareness and application of pedagogic principles in work with adults. Rogoff (2003) writes of 'intent participation' in children's motivation, where children's development occurs through their active interest in the cultural systems in which they exist. The developing interest is supported by a value-based opportunity to pur-sue that interest. This interest may be 'guided' by a more experienced other (an experienced peer or mentor). We recognize that there must be some constraints with regard to the work environment, but that on the whole, people work best when they are interested in what they are doing, and when they can look to others for support if needed. Ferre Laevers (2000) writes of children's 'involvement' as a supportive indicator of deep-level learning. Such involvement is linked to an increased sense of well-being or feeling 'at home' in the environment. As with a 'secure base', this comfort within the environment allows for a deeper exploration of chosen activities or a deeper level of 'involvement' and contingent learning. Thus, an environment which supports emotional well-being and 'intrinsic motivation' enables one to work in a more focused way towards self-acknowledged values and outcomes – themes further explored in Chapters 5 and 6.

The leader's task in an early years setting is to build on adult intrinsic motivation within a common culture of the organization – its visions and values. The leader of the early childhood setting must nurture the common understanding and assimilation in the staff team, of the setting's vision and values – what Fullan calls the 'moral base'. The leader now becomes 'the context setter, the designer of a learning experience, not an authority figure with solutions. Once the folks at the grass roots realize that they own the problem, they also discover that they can help to create and own the answer...' (Fullan, 2004: 162).

We now begin to see how we can use pedagogical principles to support an understanding of early childhood leadership, teamwork, and achievement of cohesion through change processes. The progress of a team through change experiences is one of learning. The application of pedagogical principles can support the learning environment for children and adults in the learning community represented by an early years setting. In such settings, children learn and develop towards adulthood, and adults learn to develop a growing maturity and adaptability to better support children.

In 2005, Bruce proposed a set of ten 'bedrock principles' for the early childhood practitioner (2005: 12–13) and several can be applied to leadership principles. These adapted principles are presented in Table 3.3 alongside a possible interpretation for informed leadership pedagogy.

 Point for Reflection

Try the same exercise with the principles of the Early Years Foundation Stage.

Consider: Have your staff been given the opportunity to explore and innovate, to shape and own the new practices of the organization?

Mistakes arising from attempted innovation can be seen in holding and containing organizations with a positive, no-blame perspective. The fear-based emotions of innovation can be held and contained, perhaps by other team members. The errors can be reviewed, so that learning takes place and motivation to experiment and innovate is

Table 3.3   Bruce's 'bedrock principles' (2005)

Bruce's 'Bedrock Principles' (2005)	Possible Adult Leadership Interpretation
Children are whole people who have feelings, ideas, a sense of embodied self and relationships with others, and who need to be physically, mentally, morally and spiritually healthy.	Adults as staff and team members are people who have feelings, ideas, prior knowledge, a sense of self, and relationships with others, who need to be physically, mentally, morally and spiritually healthy.
Children learn best when they are given appropriate responsibility, are allowed to experiment, make errors, decisions and choices and are respected as autonomous learners.	Adults both learn and adapt when they are given appropriate responsibility, allowed to experiment, make errors, decisions and choices and are respected as autonomous and informed practitioners.
Self-discipline is emphasized as the only kind of discipline worth having … children need their efforts to be valued and appreciated.	Self-discipline is the only kind of discipline worth having … adults need 'intent participation' for motivation, and for their efforts to be valued and appreciated.
There are times when children are especially able to learn particular things.	There are particular skills in individuals which make them especially able to support particular actions.
What children can do, rather than what they cannot, is the starting point for a child's learning.	Recognition of an adult's skill and knowledge, rather than a focus on their resistance to change, is the starting point for facilitating development and innovation.
Diverse kinds of symbolic behaviour develop and emerge when learning environments conducive to this are created through home and early childhood settings, indoors and outdoors, working together. These include pretend and role play, imagination, creativity and representations through talking/ signing, literature, writing, mathematics, dance, music, the visual arts, drama and scientific hypothesizing.	Creativity and innovation emerge in staff teams where settings have a culture of learning, dialogue and communicating, and an acceptance that there will be some errors where there is risk-taking. An open, learning culture supports the bravery of divergent thinking and creative responses, reduces the stress surrounding innovation and embraces change as part of its regenerative and creative process.

(Continued)

Table 3.3   (Continued)

Bruce's 'Bedrock Principles' (2005)	Possible Adult Leadership Interpretation
Relationships with other people (both adults and children) are of central importance in a child's life, influencing emotional and social well-being.	Positive relationships and a sense of belonging are of importance in adult employment roles, and influence their emotional and social well-being and ability to perform. Teams may be strengthened where staff support each other when things have gone wrong. Errors thus become positive team-building and formative incidents.
Quality education is about three things: the child, the context in which learning takes place, and the knowledge and understanding which the child develops and learns.	A positive and developing early childhood organization is aware of the needs of its staff and works to balance their contexts, the children's contexts and the context in which the organization is placed (the core purpose, vision and values of the setting) for a strong team.

maintained, which is preferable to the adoption of a stifling, restrictive discipline from above.

In order to understand the stifling nature of restrictive control from above, let us consider a child in the context of an early years setting. The child is involved in building with large wooden blocks. He begins by building a low wall that he has built many times before. This is a safe approach, but limited to his existing skills, without innovation. Taking a risk, he decides to build higher, and in so doing he explores new concepts. However, in unfamiliar territory, he places one brick awkwardly and the high wall falls down noisily, drawing a sharp reaction from a nearby practitioner: 'what on earth are you doing? That could be dangerous, so play sensibly'. The practitioner is authoritarian, and the child is now shocked, disappointed and considers that he is being punished for his risk-taking and innovation. He is unlikely to feel comfortable taking risks and building that high wall again. His innovation is restricted.

Practitioners have all responded to children emotively and instantly at some point. How much more constructive, but also more time-consuming, and more demanding in terms of patience, would be a response which supports the child to consider for himself what the problem was, what the solutions might be, and what to do next, without reproach. The discipline of using such patience and support with both children and adults is one of the challenges of leadership in a busy early years setting where demands on time are high.

Picture of Practice

Below is an adult situation which parallels the child example given

A member of staff decides to support free-flow play, both indoors and outdoors. It is autumn and the weather has been very wet. She has not had the practice experience of free flow from indoors to outdoors to adequately think through the implications, and neither have the children attending the setting who normally have outdoor play restricted to set times. She introduces the idea of indoor to outdoor free flow and briefly encourages the children to put on their wellies and coats when they go outside. However, during the day, the children get very enthusiastic about this new experiment and run from indoors to outdoors, taking indoor toys outside, and leaves and mud indoors. At the end of the day, all the practitioners in the room are exhausted, there is mud on the floor, toys are all over the outside area, and the cleaner has just arrived and expressed anger at the mess the room is in. The nursery manager is called to talk to the member of staff who instigated this new approach.

There are at least two possible scenarios for the nursery manager's response. In the first, the manager says, 'what on earth have you been doing? Who said that the children could be allowed to go outside whenever they want? You will have to stay and clear all this up now!' The practitioner is unsupported. She had tried something new, and was faced with punishment because it did not quite work as envisaged. She also experiences a disappointment which is not held or contained. It might also be that other practitioners distance themselves from her decision in the face of authority. She is unlikely to try to support free-flow play again outside of summer and the team has temporarily split.

A different response in the leader might have been to have taken time to consider what the practitioner was trying to do – implementing Claxton's 'slow knowing' (1997: 3). The manager may have taken the practitioner aside before speaking to her (thus leaving the team intact). She may ask what the practitioner was trying to do, what the problems were and what solutions there may be. Perhaps she will reassuringly acknowledge the disappointment in the practitioner's experience today and suggest a reprieve while further research is done. An acknowledgement of her attempt at innovation might also be appropriate. The practitioner has gained an experience and an opportunity for further learning and the environment is safe for future risk-taking. Leadership and change management issues are also ones of power and control. It is important who decides the boundaries and limitations.

Pedagogical leadership for change is therefore both leadership of pedagogical practices (a support for learning which extends throughout the organization to staff, children and families) and the use of pedagogical theory to inform leadership approaches. The management of change in early years is an obligation upon leaders as structures, systems and methods alter to best serve the core purpose of the setting (the support for children and families). In one setting, staff were so emotionally drained by the change process and concerned for their own futures that they openly acknowledged that 'the focus on the children and families has dropped during this change process' and '… it can be very easy for children to be left in limbo while practitioners deal with the business of change' (Andrews, 2007).

It is possible to support an innovative and adventurous team raising their own change challenges, and the scenarios given hold lessons to help embrace imposed change as challenge and exploration rather than an agent of disequilibrium. An organization with an established culture of questioning, lateral thinking and problem solving will be able to interpret new impositions, consider reasoned responses, and identify whether they can morally adapt to the new purpose or practice. Just as a child in an empowering setting will have that experience to enable him or her to ask questions, and look to support his or her own learning needs, so staff in a holding and containing organization which operates with moral respect will be able to ask questions, and gain support for their own professional development needs.

Picture of Practice

Empowered Innovation

In the initial Children's Centres, practitioners could shape their own jobs within the boundaries of their job descriptions. Very motivated people were actively recruited. It would have been inappropriately restricting to overtly direct their work or request that they require approval for each innovation. The Training to Employment practitioner in one Children's Centre, for example, was very skilled and knowledgeable in supporting adult participation and learning. She clearly drove her work forward for her own satisfaction. Her boundaries and limitations were set by funding, room availability and a professional morality. She clearly adopted the values of the centre, was aware of the longer-term targets, and had pride in her work. She developed some very innovative training opportunities to raise self-esteem in parents, such as developing a partnership with the local fire station and offering parents the opportunity to train with the fire service for a day. The physical challenges they experienced achieved the desired results. She received praise for her innovation from parents and staff and enjoyed logging her results so that she was able to demonstrate the impact of her work to Ofsted when it was time for the centre inspection. The centre's work with parents was identified as 'outstanding'. The centre leader's role was minimal, but the outcome successful because of both the ability of the worker and the environment in which she could explore, innovate and adapt.

Holding and Containing Organizations for Change

The ongoing development of early childhood settings as safe spaces for children and practitioners, led by an emotionally aware and magnanimous leadership, will result in settings where staff anxieties are 'held' and 'contained' but where staff are also able to innovate, learn from mistakes and develop. In this way, the staff team becomes resilient and able to understand and model the holding and containing of change anxieties in others. This approach creates 'change embracing', learning and flexible communities, who share moral purpose, deal with stress and engender 'powerful relationships' to support their work with children and families and the future sustainability of their settings. These would not be stagnant organizations, devoid of innovation, but settings which understand that there is more than one type of change. While recognizing that 'quick fix' may have a place, they also respect and understand the need for 'slow knowing', 'deep' commitment, and consistency to support steady progressive, generative and regenerative change led from within. Perhaps, with greater respect for such change management models, we can help to reduce the impact of the waves of externally imposed changes acknowledged in early childhood today.

Personal and Professional Development Activity

A slow-knowing, reflective leader is able to consider factors which help to support a change-embracing organization. Take time to consider the following questions:

- How can you create a secure base within your organization?

- How could you ensure that the organization works to 'hold' and 'contain' the anxieties of your staff?

- What are the barriers to innovation and embracing change?

- Can any imposed change be managed more appropriately?

Suggested Further Reading

Friedman, M. (2005) *Trying Hard is Not Good Enough: How to Produce Measurable Improvements for Customers and Communities.* Crewe: Trafford Publishing.

This text provides a consideration of ways to plan, implement and measure the impact of the change process from an outcome-led perspective. It is in clear language, with user-friendly models.

Fullan, M. (2004) *Leading in a Culture of Change: A Personal Action Guide and Workbook.* San Francisco: Jossey-Bass.

This book provides a facilitative perspective on moral leadership for change management, together with further personal and professional development tools in a workbook format.

Goleman, D. (2002) *The New Leaders: Transforming the Art of Leadership into the Science of Results.* London: Littlebrown.

This book is key reading for those who wish to discover more about emotionally intelligent leadership.

Handy, C. (1994) *The Empty Raincoat.* London: Arrow.

Handy argues that the sigmoid curves are the very essence of life, and that we are led by this ebb and flow, but can all play a part rather than being 'a cog in somebody else's wheel hurtling god knows where'.

4

Partnership Working in the Early Years

Michael Reed

Chapter Overview

This chapter considers ways in which professional workers can come together to provide a cohesive service to support children and families, a practice variously described as multi-agency working, collaborative working, inter-agency working or more recently partnership working. The chapter describes a number of 'driving forces' which have promoted inter-professional working and considers the benefits to children and families. It raises some key questions surrounding the subject:

- Why has the concept of partnership working become so important to those involved with early years services, including parents?
- What driving forces can be identified which promote partnership working?
- What impact does partnership working have upon the roles and responsibilities of those leading and managing partnership working?
- What can we learn from an example of partnership working within a Children's Centre?

Why Has the Concept of Partnership Working Become So Important?

Over the past ten years, there has been a rapid expansion of services to support children and families. This expansion has been driven by a desire to improve educational standards, take children out of poverty and provide the foundations upon which young children can thrive and develop. In order to meet these aims, the government introduced a framework of policies which have encouraged the workforce to develop new skills and refine existing practices. A key element in this approach was a government report, *Every Child Matters* (DfES, 2004a), paralleled in Scotland as *Getting it Right for Every Child: Proposals for Action* (The Scottish Government, 2005). Both documents highlighted the need for a trained workforce with multi-disciplinary roles and the provision of services with common goals. This stance was based upon a developing view that working in partnership could lead to an increase in children's well-being and promote improved academic attainment, as children were developing learning skills (Pettit, 2003). The work of Sloper (2004) reinforced this view and found that families with key workers to coordinate services report improved quality of life, better relationships with those providing a service, quicker access to services and reduced levels of stress for staff. A report from the National Foundation for Educational Research (NFER, 2006) found that inter-professional or multi-agency working as part of an intervention programme had a positive effect upon children and their families and that there were more positive relationships formed between professionals. Other projects also confirm similar positive outcomes, such as the work of Kurtz and James (2002) who suggest that the targeting of children's mental health and well-being via a multi-agency approach, led to a reduction in the proportion of those with clinically significant problems, as well as better engagement with school. There are also results from a report by Hallam et al. (2004) who consider inter-agency teams supporting families with children who demonstrate challenging behaviour. They report a change in self-esteem and self-worth and a reduction in school exclusions. It is also important to note that multi-agency working underpins what can be called a preventative approach to working with families and a reduction of referrals to local authority services (Yorkshire & Humber Children's Fund, 2004). The work of Atkinson et al. (2002) into multi-agency working and a further report into the impact of services (2003) also illustrate the benefits inherent within a partnership approach. Families were able to:

- access services not previously available, from a wider range of services

- gain easier or quicker access to services or expertise

- develop improved educational attainment and better engagement in education

- receive early identification and intervention

- have children's needs addressed more appropriately

- receive better quality services

- reduce their need for more specialist services.

It could be argued that these positive outcomes are in part due to increased access to childcare as part of government initiatives, which have had a considerable impact on early years services. It could be that increased training for early years practitioners has underpinned the importance of parental partnership and led to parents being more involved in their children's learning. It may be that parents are finding it easier to take up employment due to the provision of affordable childcare. It may also be that extended schools are increasingly providing more opportunity to participate in sports, arts and cultural activities; and are becoming adept at drawing upon support to meet additional needs. Perhaps, when these factors are taken together, inter-agency working may be seen as part of a whole process that is encouraging professionals to provide support for families. In effect, it is providing a single point of contact with services to help ensure quicker access to the right kind of support (Mukherjee et al., 1999).

For professional workers themselves, there are also benefits from operating a partnership approach. There are opportunities for exchanging professional expertise and for developing a holistic approach to the needs of children. There are also opportunities to develop shared values between different professions, as shared training is promoted and developed (Sure Start, 2005). This is something that Halsey et al. (2005) saw as engaging in professional development – opportunities to share expertise and learn from colleagues through discussion of casework and joint delivery of interventions. Families of vulnerable children are likely to be in contact with many different agencies and professionals – for example, health, education, social services, housing and benefits. Families with disabled children see many different professionals and some have a whole range of professionals visiting them each year (Sloper, 2004). Often, families need help in order to understand the roles and responsibilities of different agencies and professionals. They need to see that professionals work together and share common goals, and want to see 'joined up' working rather than be referred on from one agency to another. In this way, partnership working can reduce the stresses and strains associated with having to deal with a multiplicity of practitioners and alleviate stress for parents and carers.

> 〰️ **Point for Reflection**
>
> Consider the successes that professional partnership may bring and the reasons why this is advantageous to families:
>
> - more focused attention on the child and their family and less replication between different professionals
> - working together means there is likely to be a shared understanding of practice and less time spent overcoming professional barriers
> - more opportunities for shared professional development and career progression
> - more involvement in community development as part of coordinated local services
> - changing public perceptions of the way professional services will develop in the future.

Driving Forces

In order to promote and develop professional partnerships, it has been necessary to develop a reappraisal of working practices across a diverse range of early years provision. These include pre-schools that have a pivotal role in maintaining early years care and education within large sections of the community, private and community-based day nurseries, and specialist services for children with significant difficulties in accessing learning, as well as a large number of maintained schools and nurseries. Provision also includes childminders providing a flexible service for children and families, Children's Centres, assessment centres, family centres, workplace and retail crèches, and more recently after school and breakfast clubs. In addition, there are toy library services as well as 'parent and toddler groups'. Into this diverse mix, we can add professional services such as speech therapists, educational psychologists, social workers, local authority advisory staff, the inspection service, and those involved in quality assurance. There are also voluntary services (both local and national) and self-help groups. Increasingly, there are online support groups representing and responding to the needs of parents. Whether these are strictly 'settings' is an interesting question, but they represent a growing network used by parents and professionals. They encourage discussion about government directives and curriculum advice as part of online forums. There are also websites that hold and distribute information about research and the impact of services on children and families and online services to support training, such as college and university websites. Therefore, any attempt to refine existing policies amongst such a range of provision is no easy task and perhaps made more difficult because practitioners themselves have different experiences of partnership working. Some have engaged in training with practitioners in the same field, but from different settings. Some may have engaged in training or attended meetings alongside other professional groups and some may have forged links with specialist services to support the children in their care. Some may have contact with teachers, speech and language therapists, or an educational psychologist, while others may have attended case conferences or sought the support of colleagues with professional heritages steeped in the health service, social work, or community work. All are being asked to work purposefully in partnership with other professional colleagues.

It was therefore important for the government to ensure that policies, directives, and legislative changes acted as driving forces that would move partnership working into the mainstream of early years practice. They have been well documented by writers such as Baldock et al. (2005) and some key initiatives are referred to in this chapter. All contain what appears to be a genuine desire to protect the welfare of children and a realization that working together means a more efficient and cohesive framework of services for families. As Wilson and Pirric (2000) suggest, such working is in itself part of raising standards and this view was reinforced by a joint statement in 2007 from the General Social Care Council (GSCC), the General Teaching Council for England (GTC) and the Nursing and Midwifery Council (NMC). The statement makes a case for partnership working and suggests that practitioners should concern themselves with the whole child, whatever their specialism. This is a view underpinned by the Children's Workforce Strategy (DfES, 2006b, 2007b) which recognizes the importance of an integrated approach to supporting the education of children, and by the National Childcare Strategy (DfES, 2004b) which sets out the way the government would deliver on the commitments made to transform the range of childcare services available to parents. In tandem with these reports was a National Service Framework (DoH/DfES, 2004) which contained a strategy to promote a more proactive approach to children's health. The Common Assessment Framework (CAF) (DfES, 2006b) underpinned this preventative approach. The framework is intended to bring together a common form of assessment that can be utilized within a number of early years settings, such as Children's Centres, schools, early years facilities, health services, and the voluntary sector. It is intended to draw agencies together and offer a preventative and proactive approach. It does this by requiring trained professionals to take an interdependent view of providing services. This means following processes and procedures for assessment that have a common core. It starts with the unborn child and follows them into infancy, their schooling, and their development into young people. It promotes changes to the way professionals perceive roles and responsibilities and considers the need for a 'lead professional' to coordinate services. It also asks that professionals be trained to share information about the child, family, and legal processes. Indeed, the sharing of information is seen as being of paramount importance and a means of reducing inequalities between disadvantaged children and others. There is an emphasis on practitioners explaining processes clearly, realizing that the safety and welfare of the child is paramount, whenever possible respecting confidentiality when sharing information, maintaining accuracy of information, seeking advice from others, and recording the process, especially in regard to decisions made. These initiatives are enshrined in the Childcare Act 2006. It reinforces parents' expectations for the provision of high-quality childcare services and confirms the role of Local Education Authorities as leaders in forging partnership across all sectors. Partnership working is also recognized within the Children's Plan (DCSF, 2007) and the Early Years Foundation Stage (EYFS) (DfES, 2007a). Both require practitioners to have regard for the 'whole child' and collaborate with all agencies supporting the child's welfare. Practitioners must ensure continuity and coherence by the sharing of information between different settings a child attends, and it is acknowledged that practitioners will frequently need to work with professionals from other agencies.

There has also been a movement away from defining early years workers as those who 'care' for children towards those who offer professional services to assist the whole child and family. This can be seen by the adoption of an integrated qualifications framework for those working with children and families (DfES, 2006a, 2007b). It is also possible for those from a range of professional backgrounds, with relevant experience and qualifications, to gain the status of Early Years Professional (EYP) and there are nationally agreed standards for the leaders of Children's Centres (DfES, 2007c). All of these identify the need to promote integrated professional partnerships, and there are a number of training initiatives taking place at universities which focus on training practitioners from different disciplines to act together for the benefit of children at undergraduate and postgraduate levels (SWAP, 2007).

Such changes in professional expectation have been subject to much debate. Moss (2006) and Aubrey (2007) are just some of the contributors. The debate includes being concerned about developing a technocratic workforce, the need to encourage opportunities for reflection on practice and concern about the pace of change. Perhaps this adds a note of caution to the way we should consider how the government has driven forward the notion of partnership working. As well as many positive initiatives, there needs to be time set aside to take stock of such changes, consolidate good practice, and evaluate carefully the impact on children and families.

〰 Point for Reflection

It would seem that there is general agreement that partnership working is of value to the family and children within the family. The government has developed initiatives to drive forward collaborative and partnership working. What does this mean for you? Can you recognize any of these initiatives?

Have you been involved in training to implement the EYFS? What emphasis did this give to working in partnership?

Are you considering presenting yourself for Early Years Professional training or have you gained that status? What emphasis does training for this award give to partnership working?

Are there Children's Centres in your area that foster partnership working? What professional groups are located at the centre?

Have you participated in any online consultation alongside other professionals?

Are you aware of national and local policies, plan directives, and legislation to enhance children's services and support partnership working?

Are you aware of the way monitoring and evaluation of early years services will take account of the way you work in partnership with other settings and agencies?

What Factors Can Be Identified that Promote Partnership Working?

In essence, partnership working means that practitioners should promote a genuine desire to exchange information and reduce barriers that exist between agencies. This should lead to joined-up working and ultimately collaborative working. It represents what Percy-Smith (2005) sees as agencies working together within a single, often new, organizational structure. However, there is a concern that this may only lead to centre-based service delivery where professionals from different agencies work together on the one site, not necessarily in an integrated manner. This is a point revealed in the views of commentators such as Wilson and Pirrie (2000) and Cameron and Lart (2003). Professionals working together, need to be well-versed in joint planning and decision-making to draw expertise as well as services together, and take responsibility for ensuring a coordinated approach which focuses on the child and their family. In practice, this can be seen at Children's Centres which are at the heart of the strategy to deliver better outcomes for children and families. Local authorities have been given strategic responsibility for the development of Children's Centres in consultation with parents, and the private, voluntary and independent sectors. They are intended to offer good quality early learning combined with full daycare provision for children. Inclusive practice is a priority which encompasses support for children with special needs and their families. Many offer drop-in sessions and other activities for children combined with good quality teacher input and an emphasis on early learning. In addition, there may be child and family health services, including ante-natal services, and a mechanism to support parents in their home. The centres are also intended to be a focal point to develop local child-minding networks. It is planned that 2500 Children's Centres will be operational by 2008, with 3500 centres (one for every community) by 2010 (DfES, 2005b). A large proportion of centres have been developed from existing settings such as Sure Start programmes and Early Excellence Centres. They have also developed from local provision, including schools, nurseries and family centres provided by the maintained, private and voluntary sectors. At first glance, such an arrangement may seem the ideal scenario in which to facilitate partnership working. Professionals are 'co-located' on one site, they are easy to contact, have defined roles and are experienced in working with hard-to-reach families. However, for the leader of the centre, it would be unwise to see integration of services as solely to do with coordination. Just because services are 'co-located' does not mean they work seamlessly together. This is because leading and managing inter-professional groups is not just about organizing which professional does what and where. It is about joining up services so that children and families benefit. It is also about recognizing that there will be occasional disputes over professional boundaries, ideological issues, and approaches to meeting the needs of individual parents. To this end, leaders must strive to foster a genuine desire to change working practices, shed preconceived ideas and have a clear view of each professional role. For parents in the local community, this also means responding to change and sometimes changing their perspectives about availing themselves of the services on offer. They too have to come to terms with sharing information and not assuming one particular professional has the 'right answer'. They also need time to develop trust in the centre and the professionals who work there. Perhaps this tells us that any development (like the establishment of a Children's Centre within the community), however well meaning, takes time to reach those who need to be most closely involved. Leaders must beware of moving too quickly (in a time of rapid professional change) and ensure that they consolidate initiatives and carefully review how they work in practice.

The Roles and Responsibilities of Those Leading and Managing Partnership Working

Working partnerships require an understanding that families and children need to be supported as they make transitions between agencies. 'Referring on' is useful, but needs to be done with care. Just because another professional is 'close at hand' does not mean they understand. Partnership working means establishing shared practices, engendering trust between professionals and giving people the confidence to share expertise. For leaders, this does not mean trying to micro-manage every situation that comes along or becoming a 'pseudo-psychologist' for every family. It does mean having a clear commitment to sharing expertise and listening to people and most importantly developing a shared view that sees supporting children and families as the driving force that promotes working partnerships. This underpins the view of Atkinson et al. (2002) who underline the complexity and potential of developing joined-up services. For a leader, this means they must learn to speak the same professional language as their colleagues and translate things that are difficult to understand into a language that is understood by all. A leader also needs to understand that integrated working inevitably means managing a number of competing arrangements – for example, managing separate budgets when different services and even personnel are funded through separate streams. A further challenge is establishing performance management structures for a disparate professional workforce such as health visitors, community workers, speech and language therapists, and teachers – finding ways for different professionals to derive ownership of policies and evolve joint working practices. This may mean setting up a forum such as a community board for all key partners, including education, health, social services, the police, local business, and charities to identify priorities, and commit to working in partnership. Alongside these procedures and structures, a leader also has to display the human face of leadership. This means supporting 'people' as well as their 'professional role' and finding time to respond to queries and concerns. It also means having on occasions to make difficult decisions about the value and validity of particular services. This requires more than intuition and a leader must have in place robust strategies to monitor and refine services as necessary. This includes an awareness of the range of external inspection services that may operate within different professional contexts as well as local accreditation programmes for quality assurance.

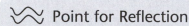 Point for Reflection

It is now possible to draw together a view of the personal skills and leadership qualities necessary to foster partnership working. As you look at these, think about the complex role inherent in serving the needs of families. This means not only being aware of what services are available and ways to foster partnership working, but at the same time promoting independence and reducing professional dependency.

Personal skills and leadership qualities

A good leader should:

- become well-versed in many of the working practices seen as determining success for integrated services. This means keeping up to date and being aware of professional resources available in the wider community
- have a clear knowledge of where professional colleagues are located and how to approach them, understanding their roles,

responsibilities and what they too expect from any professional relationship

- develop an understanding about the professional heritages that exist within integrated teams – how other professionals are trained and their working practices
- have in place effective ways to transfer (between those most closely involved) information about children and families
- engage in and develop 'joint training' initiatives and use online services provided by local authorities, colleges and universities to share views, opinions and expertise
- be aware of the expertise and strengths within professional teams and facilitate ways of allowing team members to share that expertise and recognize each other's strengths
- provide strong leadership and good systems of information
- recruit people with skills and experience of partnership working
- provide simple and clear policies that underpin and value partnership working
- monitor whether policies are being implemented and where necessary refine, change and update policies in practice
- encourage colleagues to take the initiative and to innovate
- coordinate and align services for maximum impact
- agree standardized procedures as far as possible, to reduce potential conflict between agencies and different professional procedures
- give time to translating the languages used by different professional groups into a language understood by all.

This list is not complete as it is accepted that practitioners need to continually reflect and learn from commentators and researchers who have investigated the process of partnership or integrated working – for example, see the work of Boddy et al. (2006), who explored models of practice for children with special educational needs, and the work of Aubrey (2007). She tells us that leadership and management need to be more clearly understood and identifies a range of issues that will encompass early years leadership and management in the future. She suggests that the role of early childhood leaders has become evermore challenging and that we need to have a better understanding of the relationship between different models of multi-agency working and positive outcomes for children. Aubrey argues that it is unlikely that any one single leadership approach can be appropriate for such a diverse sector; in other words, flexible leadership is the key. On the ground, this means that there may be diverse models of practice. In particular, the role of the leader may take a number of different forms. There is also a delicate balance between encouraging partnership and the resulting increase in workload on all involved. Therefore, leaders must carefully monitor the opportunities and constraints that partnership working brings.

A Picture of Practice set within a Children's Centre

This picture of practice comes from the work of practitioners based in a Children's Centre. It represents practice that is being refined and adapted in order to meet the needs of families. It is not meant to represent the *only* way to work in partnership; it is a snapshot of *developing* practice.

The Children's Centre is located in a market town in a rural 'shire' county of England. It serves a community that is diverse in terms of family income, take up of educational opportunities and cultural heritage. It was purpose-built as a Children's Centre in 2004 and is situated next to a successful primary school. Most families who use the centre live in houses built as part of an estate in the 1970s. The centre is part of the local community and presents a welcoming environment for families. There is parking for cars, but walking is encouraged along a series of wide pathways leading to an area where prams can be stored securely. As you enter, there is a foyer, large enough to provide not only pram and wheelchair access but also a space to pick up information, talk to a receptionist and gain entry into the main building. This appears to be such a simple aspect of the 'environment' but was clearly constructed to meet the needs of parents who may well have two young children, bags of shopping and need to speak to the receptionist to confirm a visit or just find out useful information.

Figure 4.1 illustrates the way the centre views its work as firmly based around the child and the family. It has the child and family at its core and shows the range of services available rather than the nature and roles of the professionals working at the centre. This is important, because the primary focus of the Children's Centre is on the delivery of services. For some families, this means their main contact with the centre is the sessional nursery or daycare centre. Others may access services as diverse as the young parents group and baby massage. From time to time, however, parents may need to move into the orbit of many other services according to their particular needs. This may stem from the parents themselves or from a professional worker in consultation with colleagues at the centre. This again illustrates the ethos of the centre, which encourages sharing information, reducing professional barriers, and seeing professional expertise as something that collectively works for the benefit of parents and children. Such an approach also encompasses a desire to see the range of

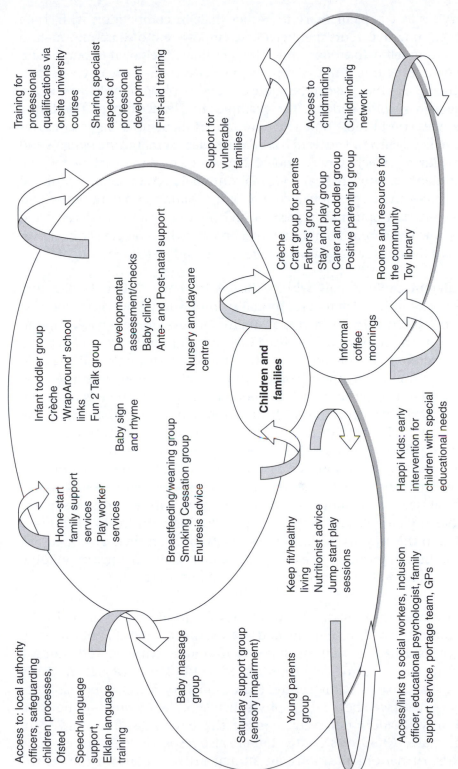

Figure 4.1 A 'map' of the Children's Centre

services as complementary to, rather than in competition with, each other. Indeed, parents themselves are empowered to share information and form self-help groups, which then facilitate their own resources, and draw in expertise. If this all sounds too 'perfect', there are of course particular issues that have to be addressed and resolved in order to encourage partnership working. For example, the leadership of the centre requires considerable time and effort and is made up of representatives from key agencies. The team has become adept at managing budgets and prioritizing which service should be extended, developed or refined. Inevitably, this means that there is a continual need to obtain additional resources and to promote a culture of innovation and continuing professional development. Unquestionably, this leads to a more educated and informed workforce, but it means that on many occasions, expertise moves out of the centre as qualifications are gained and preferment sought.

Different professionals within the centre have different roles and responsibilities. There are specialist professional workers such as health visitors who have responsibility for developmental assessment. Staff in the nursery offer advice on education and care and act as a pivotal point for collaboration with others – for example, liaising with the community support worker who has direct input into the early years resource centre which includes a toy library. There is a teacher who works in partnership with all members of the multi-agency team. She works closely with the speech and language service, has a role in forging links with local schools and plays a significant part in shaping the educational philosophy of the nursery. Centre staff also include specialist portage workers, who support children with special educational needs, and staff who coordinate work with parents to support a healthy lifestyle and deepen communication with the local community. In this way, individual professionals focus on their own specialist area but, importantly, each professional plays a role in guiding parents towards a particular service as appropriate.

The centre also creates opportunities for local employment in the community and in so doing adds new skills to a local labour market. It plays a part in training staff via in-house seminars and training events and a university-coordinated Foundation Degree in Early Years, also based at the centre. Professional roles and responsibilities also extend well beyond the physical area of the centre into the community. Leaders not only manage the day-to-day running of an Integrated Children's Centre, but are also responsible for developing, with partner organizations, an annual delivery plan for the centre, and leading the implementation of this plan. They must also provide

Partnership working represents the whole learning community for the children and their families

a robust evaluation programme and regularly evaluate the work of the centre and its impact on the lives of parents and children. Added to this is the responsibility for the centre budget in accordance with internal and external audit requirements. There is also the production of regular financial reports and a requirement for ensuring that the work of the centre complies with legislative and regulatory demands. Permeating all of these duties is an awareness of the centre leadership that they must ensure that equal opportunities and inclusion issues are considered within the centre and the community.

Professionals working at the centre have evolved ways to deal with such disparate demands and there is a genuine attempt to enact the vision of the centre, which is to offer support, advice and care to all children and families in the local community. They see this as a process, not a series of events or targets, though realize that from time to time, there are inevitably going to be disputes over professional decisions, ideological issues and approaches to meeting the needs of individual parents. Nevertheless, it would be realistic to suggest that partnership working works well at the centre. Overall, this is because professionals give of their time to make things work. Above all, they demonstrate a willingness to change working practices and share expertise with the aim of supporting children and families in the community.

Summary

This chapter has introduced many concepts and issues associated with professional partnership and changes in practice. When you consider the impact of these changes, think about changing roles, responsibilities and relationships. Also, think about the diversity of early years provision in which change takes place and the experience of those most closely involved. View the changes as part of a mechanism that is gradually altering the way we perceive working together for the benefit of children. In particular, think about the way the chapter has:

- suggested how partnership working underpins the way professionals are able to support, protect and safeguard vulnerable children and families
- considered how the leadership, management and coordination of integrated services are evolving
- identified opportunities and constraints that someone managing and leading an early years setting needs to consider when introducing changes in working practices
- recognized the differences in professional experience and individual perspectives about partnership working that the leader may hold
- underlined the importance of recognizing that partnership working is for the benefit of families. It has to be managed and coordinated effectively
- revealed examples of positive professional practice to support such working – in particular, the roles and responsibilities of those most closely involved
- highlighted the way that Children's Centres are becoming the focus for partnership working
- argued that all professionals need to view partnership working as an essential part of their role.

Personal and Professional Development Activity

Below is a short exercise that may prompt you to consider issues surrounding the developing role of Children's Centres and partnership working. This may prove useful in assisting your studies or allowing you to reflect on practice. Look at the 'positive actions' set out below. These describe actions that you might take in order to promote partnership working. You should view these from your own perspective and relate them to your setting. Think about short, medium and longer-term aims for each.

As an example, point number 3 asks you to consider an action that promotes a unified view of professional practice. In the longer term, this might mean electing to be part of a group that brings together colleagues from different disciplines to develop a shared view of practice. This could be as part of regular meetings at a Children's Centre. Over the medium term, it could mean engaging in shared inter-professional training in your area, probably linked to the working of a local Children's Centre. In the short term, it could mean using the internet to find out more about a particular discipline or locating additional information about the work of Children's Centres. When you formulate your response, try to concentrate on 'actions' which allow you to forge positive relationships with other professionals.

Short term   –   in the next few weeks

Medium term –   within two or three months

Long term   –   over three school terms or up to a year

Consider:

1   an action that helps you to understand different professional practice

2   an action that brings you into direct contact with a local Children's Centre to find out what services they provide for parents

3   an action that promotes a unified view of professional practice

4   an action to promote the sharing of information between professionals

5   an action to promote (and share) with different professionals the opportunity (for them) to see what you do as part of your professional role

6   an action which is decisive – making an informed decision to enable partnership working – as a member of, (for example) a governing body, as an Early Years Professional or a leader

7   an action that focuses on ways to inform parents about different professional services for maximum impact on families and children.

Suggested Further Reading and Electronic Sources

Laming, H. (2003) *The Victoria Climbié Inquiry*. Available from: www.victoria-climbie-inquiry.org.uk/

This is essential reading in relation to understanding why it is important to work in professional partnership to safeguard the welfare of children.

Paige-Smith, A. and Craft, A. (eds) (2007) *Developing Reflective Practice in the Early Years*. Milton Keynes: Open University Press.

This book provides a comprehensive view of professional practice. It underlines the importance of reflection on practice to improve professional development.

www.northumberland.gov.uk
This website provides details of local authority integrated services for children and examples of practice.

SWAP: Social Policy and Social Work Subject Centre University of Southampton, Southampton, S017 1BJ

www.swap.ac.uk
This website considers research into inter-professional practice, professional collaboration, and the development of training to facilitate inter-agency working.

5

Making a Positive Contribution

Melanie Pilcher

Chapter Overview

This chapter considers group dynamics and the facilitation of team building as a means to encourage the development of positive motivation and attitudes. The team is defined in terms of children, practitioners and parents, identifying the roles and responsibilities of each and discussing the importance of collaborative working to enable positive contributions. Potential difficulties and barriers are explored alongside the importance of emotional literacy to the effective operation of teams. Consideration of the children's contribution to provision focuses on strategies for listening to the child's voice.

First Principles

In order to secure the best possible outcomes for children and families, it is essential that those involved in their welfare and development can work together and, most importantly, feel that they are able to make a positive contribution. Collaborative working is a strong theme throughout this book and is explored with different emphasis in other chapters. In *Every Child Matters: Change for Children* (DfES, 2004a) and its underpinning legislation in the Children Act (2004d), the government set out aims to help all children and young people achieve five outcomes that they identified as being the most important: being healthy, staying safe, enjoying and achieving, making a positive contribution and achieving economic well-being. This meant that the practitioners and organizations involved in providing services for children would be working together and sharing information, thus making a positive contribution themselves. These outcomes are further supported by the pioneering Childcare Act (2006), the first piece of legislation concerned exclusively with early years and childcare in England which aims to continue the whole system transformation of children's services, both locally and nationally. Similarly, Scotland, Wales and Northern Ireland are putting an emphasis on collaborative working that truly involves children, parents, practitioners, agencies and other partners. Each nation has appointed a children's commissioner to give children and young people a voice in government and public life. In March 2005, the first Children's Commissioner for England was appointed. The role of the commissioner is to listen to and put forward the views of children and young people, including those who are most vulnerable in our society, and to ensure their involvement in the work of organizations whose decisions and actions affect them.

True collaboration involves working together, sharing tasks and listening to each other

The Early Years Foundation Stage (EYFS) introduced in September 2008 (DfES, 2007a) replaces the Birth to Three Matters framework DfES (2002), the Curriculum Guidance for the Foundation Stage (DfES, 2000), and the National Standards for Under 8s Daycare and Childminding (DfES, 2003a), and reflects these outcomes throughout with four guiding themes that work together to underpin effective practice in its delivery. The four themes of the EYFS are:

- **A Unique Child** – every child is a competent learner from birth who can be resilient, capable, competent and self-assured.

- **Positive Relationships** – children learn to be strong and independent from a base of loving and secure relationships with parents and/or a key person.

- **Enabling Environments** – the environment plays a key role in supporting and extending children's development and learning.

- **Learning and Development** – children develop and learn in different ways and at different rates, and all areas of learning and development are equally important and interconnected.

There is much emphasis on partnership in the EYFS as well as in other initiatives that impact on the lives of children, families and early years practitioners. For example, *Every Parent Matters* (DfES, 2007d), which places even greater emphasis on the need for practitioners to work in partnership with parents to support them as active participants in their child's learning. It is therefore worth considering just who is involved in this process and how they should be working together as a team. Within the context of this chapter, the team is seen as encompassing practitioners, children and their families. The terms 'leader and manager' are used to describe team leaders and officers in charge, while acknowledging the close relationship between the processes of leadership and management. The potential contribution and expectations of each are explored in more detail throughout the text.

What Is a Team?

In the most basic terms, a team could be described as a group of people who are connected by a common purpose or goal. These people may have been carefully selected to be part of the team because of their individual skills or knowledge, or perhaps they are a member by association because they have some involvement in one or more aspects of the team's function. In early years and childcare, a team is usually considered to be made up of those who are responsible for providing care and education in a range of settings across the private, voluntary, independent and maintained sectors. Childminders and home childcarers can also be considered teams once the children, their parents and other agencies are added to the equation. As the increasing role of the 'multi-agency team' is acknowledged and addressed in Chapter 4, consideration of the 'team' in this chapter will be based upon that already defined here and the relationships contained within it.

The common purpose of teams in early years and childcare can be broadly described as working in partnership with each other to achieve set outcomes. What becomes more complex is the reason for an individual's involvement, the level of involvement and how this is managed in order that a group of people with a common link are able to function effectively as a team.

When looking more closely at teams in early years and childcare, we find that we have people who choose to work in the team – *practitioners*, people who choose to use the services of the team – *parents*, and people for whom the team exists and are directly affected by its actions – *children*. The paradox is that historically it is the children who, while being the beneficiaries of the work of the team, have actually had the least input. Consideration of the 'child's voice' and what this really means will be considered later in this chapter.

Every Child Matters (DfES, 2004a) was one of the first pieces of work that saw the opinions and views of children being used to influence policy and change practice within the sector. The Children Act (1989) placed emphasis on seeking the views of children as appropriate to their age and understanding with regard to what happens to them; while the United Convention on the Rights of the Child (1989), Article 12, states that children should be given the right to express their own views where they are capable of doing so, in all matters that affect them. The EYFS provides a supportive framework with its overarching aim that young children are helped to achieve the five Every Child Matters outcomes. It keeps the 'uniqueness' of children at its heart, ensuring that every child is included and that learning and development begin and end with the child.

How Do Teams Develop?

Many people are familiar with Tuckman's (cited in Colenso, 1997: 22) Forming, Storming, Norming, Performing model of team development, described as the process by which a group of people become a functioning team as they go through each stage. A brief summary is given here. At the *Forming* stage, new teams are dependent on direction and guidance from a leader; individual roles and responsibilities are not yet clear. *Storming* involves team members establishing themselves through challenging the leader and each other; relationships and emotions can become contentious issues at this stage. As *Norming* takes place, there is cohesiveness which enables new roles and responsibilities to develop. When the team reaches the *Performing* stage, they will have a shared vision and are able to address interpersonal issues cohesively. Tuckman also suggests a final stage of *Adjourning*, once the work of the team is done, suggesting a beginning and end to team development.

Tuckman's model is a valuable tool for leaders and team members, all of whom need to understand where they are in the process in order to see a way forward. This is particularly important in the Storming stage when the team will have different opinions about how they should operate and different personalities will begin to emerge. This stage may also become the point at which the relationship between parents and the rest of the team is most vulnerable. The Storming process will either cement a positive relationship where parents feel fully involved, or leave them isolated, compromising any potential for true partnership. Features of this process are acknowledged in Chapter 7. The successful transition to the Performing stage involves the team actively listening to each other and accepting individual strengths and weaknesses as they find ways to work together. The individuality of the team can then be utilized to its full potential as tasks are distributed accordingly and everyone has the opportunity to contribute.

A further developmental model for a team of early years practitioners and parents is suggested within this chapter as: *Establishing, Maintaining and Collaborating.* A cyclical approach or a meta-cycle within the Performing and Norming stages of Tuckman's model, whereby the team constantly evolves but change is not perceived as a threat, it is instead accepted as being integral to continued quality improvement within the work of the team. The ideals of inspirational leadership that are put forward in Chapter 2 facilitate each of the steps by recognizing the value of individual contributions in strengthening and empowering the whole team.

Establishing

Once together, the team sets its own direction, aims are established and shared. Members take ownership of the aims and understand their roles and responsibility. When new people join, they will probably have been chosen for specific skills that enhance the work of the team. Parents are involved and are made to feel that their contributions are both welcome and important; furthermore, efforts are made to identify and overcome barriers to their participation which may be due to the unique needs of their particular community, locality or culture. New goals and targets are communicated and most importantly discussed. Change is welcomed and understood as being a necessary process that, if well managed, will enhance the work of the team.

Maintaining

The manager or leader understands the needs of the team and addresses these pro-actively. Team members are able to express themselves with confidence and respond to the emotional needs of others within the team and there is an acceptance and tolerance of differences. Such practice contributes to what Goleman (1996) describes as 'emotional literacy', thus building an ethos of mutual support and partnership that is apparent to new members. It is also easier for new members to establish a place within the team because they are not seen as a threat to the status quo which is often the perception when teams have been established for some time.

Collaborating

The team is functioning together and can now collaborate, identifying and setting new goals, or responding to those set by national policy. Empathy and sensitivity within the team facilitate dialogue that is unambiguous as individuals are able to express themselves clearly. Parental involvement is not contrived; all members of the team (including parents themselves) understand the importance of active participation in their child's learning and development. Motivation comes from within the team; they are empowered to see opportunities for, and then to initiate, change as they work together to identify and address each other's needs and those of stakeholders such as regulatory bodies or partner agencies. The team is now in the best possible position to exceed expectations set either internally or from outside and to secure the best possible outcomes.

Group Dynamics and Emotional Literacy

Whatever the reason for a team coming together, one thing is sure – teamwork rarely, if ever, just happens. Forces and interactions known as 'group dynamics' occur when individuals come together with their own ideals and perceptions of themselves and others. The complexities of group dynamics have a significant impact on how well these individuals are able to function as a team. Lewin cited in Smith (2001: online) believed that: 'Any normal group, and certainly any developed and organized one, contains and should contain individuals of very different character'. He claims that while people come together with very different dispositions, if they share a common objective, they are more likely to achieve it. Chapter 1 explores this concept further, highlighting the importance of a value-based and principled approach which, when developed both collectively and individually, contributes to the overall success of the team. However, the sharing of common objectives is not always enough to secure success – there is the potential for group dynamics to become so problematic that objectives are lost as the team struggles to find ways to work together. The manager or team leader expends time and energy in a mediative role and ultimately the productivity of the team is compromised or may stall completely.

So-called 'issues' or 'personality clashes' between parents and other members of the team are particularly damaging as they can ultimately lead to the child being removed to a new provision, even though the 'problems' have not impacted on the child's welfare and development. The following example highlights how the force of group dynamics should never be underestimated, when individuals within the group misunderstand each other and then perpetuate that misunderstanding to others within the team.

〰 Point for Reflection

Peter is an older parent whose 23-month-old son attends nursery three days a week. He has grandchildren who are older than his son and is less likely to seek guidance from nursery staff, often commenting that they themselves are 'too young' to give him advice about bringing up children. This somewhat pragmatic attitude and a hearing impairment which means that he often shouts or appears to ignore things that are said to him has led to some of the younger staff commenting that he 'looks down on them' or does not value their professionalism. In short, he is not very popular with the staff. His reputation as a difficult parent is passed on to the next group his son moves into. Staff appear to expect the worst from him, although Peter has never been rude to a member of staff and always thanks them for looking after his son each day.

Peter often refers to his son as 'his lordship' and one day refers to the nursery manager as 'her ladyship'. Staff are quick to report this

(Continued)

(Continued)

to her, making it sound as though he was being deliberately detrimental. The manager decides it's time to put Peter in his place and sends him a formal letter reminding him that she is in a position of authority and that his attitude will not be tolerated. Peter is very surprised to receive the letter, so asks to see the manager and tells her that she has a very poor attitude herself and that if he does not receive an apology, he will find a new nursery. The manager replies that she will be terminating their contract anyway. Peter decides to take the matter further and contacts Ofsted.

So many misunderstandings between Peter and the nursery staff could have been avoided with the application of emotional intelligence. Goleman describes how the ability to see things from another's perspective 'breaks down biased stereotypes, and so breeds tolerance and acceptance of differences' (1996: 285). Peter's attitude was not deliberately rude; he was considerably older than most of the other parents and some staff did not know how to relate to him. They forgot that he was hearing-impaired, and that sometimes when they chatted to him without making eye contact, he genuinely did not hear them. They labelled him as being ignorant or rude and became overly defensive to any comments he made. The manager acted upon staff concerns, but may on reflection have handled the situation differently.

Among the complexities of group dynamics, there are some assumptions that it is safe to make about practitioners in early years and childcare. They will probably be women (less than 10,000 men were working in childcare occupations in spring 2003, compared with 297,000 women according to the Equal Opportunities Commission (2004)); they are likely to choose childcare as an occupation because they have a strong desire to work with children; and finally they will care deeply about the outcomes of their work for those who are the beneficiaries of it (children and families). Indeed, recruitment campaigns have used slogans such as 'do something you love for a living' and 'make a difference', further indicating that there is an unprecedented level of emotional involvement in working with children that is not found in many other occupations. It is therefore probable that group dynamics have the potential to be emotionally charged when individuals with strong values and principles come together as a team despite the commonalities of goals and purpose. When it is a multi-agency team, the dynamics are different again, as roles and responsibilities cross over and individuals within different groups set their own boundaries and expectations of each other. Professional rivalries or 'hierarchy' can be an added complication.

It is essential that roles and responsibilities are clearly communicated within the group and to outsiders; this will help to define formal expectations. Mullins (1993) stresses the importance of role definition which is prescribed through rules, regulations and contracts of employment. Mullins also draws attention to informal expectations, which might include 'general conduct, mutual support to co-members, attitudes towards superiors and means of communicating'; he warns that when formal or informal roles are not clearly defined, then 'role conflict' can arise where individuals are not suited to the role they have been assigned, or are not clear about the requirements of the role. This must be distinguished from conflict within the group caused by clashes in personality. Group dynamics could also be compromised for some of the following reasons:

- a lack of shared vision which could lead to disputes between individuals or cause the group to lose focus

- how individuals within the group see themselves and others

- poor management or leadership, whereby 'issues' are not dealt with and the status of the leader is undermined

- the needs of individual members not being met, or additional burdens being created for the team because of a lack of emotional literacy

- lack of resources, including staff or finances, which may lead to the group competing with each other

- outside influences which could include friction with other groups

- a change of policy direction or new initiatives which require the team to reassess their beliefs and values.

For each of the problems mentioned, the same core principles apply. The group who are functioning as a team, and are 'collaborating' emotionally and operationally, are best placed to overcome challenges and are willing to accept that 'teamwork' must be 'worked at' in order that balance and harmony are maintained.

Pause for Thought

Can you think of a situation where the values and beliefs of the group or team could be compromised through a change in direction of government policy? How can this be managed to ensure that the team continues to perform?

A concern for the manager or leader will be that the group are able to cooperate with each other and other groups in order to carry out their responsibilities. Effective leadership will be required both to maintain the status quo among the team and to manage disharmony, caused by personality or role conflict.

Managers and leaders in early years have often declared themselves to be practitioners first and business people second, which is why it is suggested here that they will probably possess a strong capacity for what Goleman describes as 'managing with the heart', where emotional intelligence is applied and leadership is 'not domination, but the art of persuading people to work towards a common goal' (1996: 149). If this is the case, then the application of emotional intelligence and development of emotional literacy within the team should be a natural tendency and especially effective within the early years sector.

Positive Motivation and Quality Improvement

It is easier to motivate a team that is functioning well and achieving because success breeds motivation and motivation secures success. Positive experience reinforces our learning and makes us more likely to seek new experiences again; although it must never be suggested that success within a team should be taken for granted if it becomes the norm. It can be too easy in early years to measure ultimate success by outstanding inspection judgments or quality assurance schemes. Such schemes are known to be effective at raising the quality in settings, but can imply that once a set level is reached, then 'we are as good as we can be'. If that is the case, then where is the motivation to try harder or to seek new challenges?

The National Quality Improvement Network (NQIN) funded by the Department for Children, Schools and Families (DCFS) has produced a set of good practice principles for quality improvement processes that has an emphasis on a whole setting approach to quality in the early years. Quality improvement is described as 'a journey towards ever higher quality, involving teamwork, commitment and some thorough self-examination of practice' (NQIN, 2007: 7). Quality improvement and the positive motivation of the whole team are therefore fundamental to each other.

Self-motivation for every person within a team is a good starting point, but if this is not communicated to peers, then the individual can become isolated, believing that ultimate goals are not shared and that he/she must 'go it alone', setting their own agenda in order to be successful. Team motivation, as previously mentioned, can arise from shared successes, but is also the means by which they are attained in the first place. Quality improvements should be obvious to everyone – children, parents and staff.

 Pause for Thought

What do you think is the difference between quality improvement and quality assurance? Consider the concept of quality improvement in enabling practitioners to 'make changes to the way they think and feel about their work' (NQIN, 2007: 18). How might this impact on the leader's role?

The ideal situation is to have a team who share a vision for quality and are self-motivated, but sometimes there is a tendency to label individuals within the team as being difficult, lacking in motivation, or 'not team players', without giving due consideration as to why this might be. In our work with children, we know that this is a dangerous precedent. Children should never be labelled and their behaviour must be managed sensitively with insight and understanding from their carers. The so-called 'naughty' child is often a child whose needs are not being met; it would therefore be fair to suggest that the 'difficult' member of the team might also not have their needs being met within the work environment. Maybe the member of staff who is constantly late for the early shift and appears distracted throughout the morning is actually finding it hard to organize her own childcare needs.

Behaviour management strategies such as the Antecedent, Behaviour and Consequences (ABC) model are very effective when applied to challenging situations with children. This model is based on observations of what happens immediately prior to the behaviour, the *antecedents*; what actually happens, the *behaviour*; and then what happens immediately after the behaviour, the *consequences*. Lo and Henderson (2007) explain how the ABC model can be used to organize information and allow us to consider what has happened and what might be causing the behaviour. It could also prove helpful to apply a similar model of behaviour management to so-called 'difficult' adults, acknowledging that some behaviour might be deeply rooted and consequently not as straightforward. The following picture of practice illustrates a situation between a newly appointed manager and her deputy, where the ABC model applied informally helped the new manager to develop an understanding about the needs of her deputy from which they were both able to move forward and develop a working relationship.

Picture of Practice

A deputy in a workplace nursery has been acting as manager following the resignation of her predecessor. A recruitment freeze within the organization means that a permanent new manager is not likely to be appointed for several months. The deputy undertakes the role but tells her colleagues that she does not want the job and will be relieved when a new manager is appointed. Problems within the team, caused by uncertainties about their future sustainability and other issues such as lack of resources and training needs, are not addressed by the deputy as acting manager who tells staff that she needs their cooperation as she strives to manage the day-to-day running under duress.

A new manager is unexpectedly found in another area of the organization and is seconded to the position with very little notice. The staff and parents are generally welcoming but there are problems for the new manager as the deputy will not relinquish tasks and redefines her role as being that of joint manager, despite the fact that she is no longer supernumerary and should focus on her role as 'room leader'.

In her first few weeks, the new manager tries hard to get to know her staff and parents by involving herself in the day-to-day issues of each group. The deputy meanwhile intercepts staff and parents' queries and problems and continues to organize events and take some major decisions that would normally fall to the manager.

Initial assumptions made by the manager were that the deputy was jealous and was deliberately trying to undermine her authority. Their relationship was put under a great deal of strain as the nursery was busy and staff shortages meant that there was little time to review their expectations of each other. The new manager found herself having to be very blunt with the deputy, who subsequently became increasingly upset and this further compromised their relationship.

Reflection, assisted by the ABC model and the application of emotional intelligence through empathy, gave rise to the manager's conclusion that the behaviour was not actually hostile but was rooted in insecurity. There had been no realignment of the deputy's role, there were several things that she had excelled at as manager and would have liked to continue with; she also felt that she needed to 'protect' the other staff from what she perceived as being the threat of new leadership and other changes that were likely to occur.

Applying a very basic ABC model identified specific examples of behaviour which were then considered further by the manager before being used as a basis for discussion with the deputy.

Figure 5.1   The ABC Model

Antecedent	Behaviour	Consequence
A member of staff requests time off for a dental appointment.	The deputy authorizes this, without checking rotas drawn up by the manager, and this leaves the group short-staffed on the manager's late shift.	The staff policy clearly states that appointments must be taken (when possible) outside work hours. Other staff now feel that they have been unfairly treated in the past when time off for appointments has been refused – they are resentful towards the manager and their colleague.
Planning for the children's summer show is under way and all members of staff are involved. In the past, families have been invited.	The deputy decides that siblings will not be allowed to attend this year because of problems the year before where younger children disrupted the play. She sends a letter to parents stating this.	Parents are very upset. The manager, who does not agree with this decision, overturns it. The deputy feels that she has been made to look 'small' in front of staff and parents.
There has been a disagreement between two members of staff. One is threatening to leave.	The deputy does not tell the manager and sides with one member of staff.	The situation escalates until the alienated member of staff complains to the manager that she is being victimized and makes an official complaint.

Once the manager and deputy had set aside time to discuss roles and responsibilities against their job descriptions and set some shared targets for a working relationship, it was easier for the manager to highlight exactly when the deputy had acted inappropriately and how this had caused difficulties in the day-to-day running of the nursery. Finding a solution to the problem of how they should work together then became a collaborative exercise. The manager and deputy learnt from each other's experiences and were both able to take ownership of solutions.

 Point for Reflection

What might be the effects of a poor relationship between the manager and deputy on:

(a) the staff?
(b) the children?
(c) the parents?

In the scenario between the manager and deputy, it was the application of emotional intelligence that enabled the manager to identify the feelings of the deputy and to overcome her own impulse to react negatively towards her. It has already been suggested here that people who work with children are able to be emotionally literate in a team because of the personal traits associated with work in early years and childcare. In the early years sector, many people who would describe themselves as carers first have had to adopt a pragmatic approach to management as they have found themselves undertaking a role that is evermore business-like. Employers find that it is a challenge to appoint a manager with the right balance of business acumen and early years values and beliefs. It is often said that it is a huge challenge to deliver high quality, sustainable services for children and families within a model of good business practice when the needs of children and families are compromised by financial matters! Duffy and Marshall (2007: 109), writing about multi agency work, pose the question: 'can you effectively lead a service if you do not understand it deeply?' Chapter 4 considers the driving forces that underpin partnership working and the impact that it has upon those in leadership and management roles. In early years and childcare, it is not just about understanding the service, but understanding the needs of those accessing the service, and the needs of those working in it.

The Impact of Management Styles on the Team

Managers and leaders should be aware of management style and the impact this can have upon a team. Again, it is the application of emotional intelligence that will facilitate this process. It would probably be very difficult for an individual to completely change their management persona, but with self-awareness and a willingness to be flexible in their approach to different situations, they will be most effective. This section will focus on the potential impact of three management styles described by Mullins (1993: 243).

- **The authoritarian style** where the manager holds all the power, makes decisions, determines objectives and how they will be met.

- **The democratic style** where the group or team share leadership functions and work collaboratively in setting and working towards goals.

- **A genuine laissez-faire style** where the manager believes that the group can work well on their own and are given freedom of action with no interference, unless help is needed.

The **authoritarian** manager might be unsure of their own capacity to manage or conversely believe that nobody could do the job as well as themselves and therefore will not delegate. Staff could find this style of management disempowering, although a team who were in the early stages of 'forming' may benefit from what could be termed 'strong leadership'. The danger of an authoritarian style is that the team becomes flawed at the 'norming' and 'performing' stages because success is dependent upon one person taking the right actions. On the other hand, a team who are failing, for whatever reason, might need an authoritarian approach to maintain them until such a time that they begin to perform again.

The **democratic** style suggests participation and harmony, but it could be argued that it is most vulnerable to the forces of group dynamics that have already been discussed, because the power lies with the team. A successful democratic manager will know when to exert authority and can identify times when they must stand out from the rest of the team as 'leader'. The attributes of a democratic manager such as collaboration and team spirit would facilitate the emotional literacy of the team, but could have a negative effect if it does not allow individuals to 'shine'.

Genuine **laissez-faire** management is sometimes described as being lazy or, as Mullins suggests, 'an abdication of the responsibilities of leadership' (1993: 243). There could be several reasons for this, one of which could be that the manager believes that the team are capable of getting on with the task and will ask for help if they need it. This is fine if the team can identify that they need support, but is problematic if the manager has distanced themselves to such a point that they have no idea what the needs of the team are. It is most likely that there is little or no emotional literacy involved with this style. Alternatively, there may be a manager who appears laissez-faire because they simply do not care.

Parents and staff can be alienated by a manager or leader, whichever style is displayed. The authoritarian manager would instil confidence in those who need to see structure and order, but authority can also be very unsettling for those who are concerned that somebody else will take over and they will be steered in a direction they do not want to go. For many families who need extra support, authority can suggest unwelcome interference. Such families are more likely to seek advice and support from somebody they can relate to and who will listen to them without passing judgment or making decisions on their behalf. They need to feel confident in the knowledge and abilities of the person who is in charge but must feel able to approach them in the first place.

At the other end of the scale, the laissez-faire approach could see staff and parents taking advantage because there are no boundaries or expectations set. If the team, including parents, perceive that the manager is not fully involved, they will not feel the need to be involved themselves. There may be little emphasis placed on collaboration because it implies more work for the manager. The EYFS places great emphasis on creating a framework for partnership working between parents and professionals. It would be hard to imagine how a laissez-faire approach would facilitate this in some circumstances.

The following example will prompt discussion about how the three styles can affect the relationship between a parent and the setting.

Picture of Practice

Sandra is a young mum with two children at pre-school. She has been struggling financially for some time and her youngest child is not sleeping well. Sandra has had to take a lot of time off work because her children have been ill. She is worried about her job because she is under pressure to change her shift pattern, but the pre-school is very busy and she does not think the staff will let her change her hours. Sandra is worried that people will think she is a bad mother.

Using this example, consider how Sandra might react to different management styles and how they in turn might respond to her needs.

The Voice of the Child

This chapter begins and ends with the child and rightly so. It has already been stated here that the team exists because of the child and that historically children have had little say in matters concerning them. The emphasis of this chapter has been to encourage a holistic view of the team that includes families and children as participants and not just beneficiaries in the work of the team.

There are still some challenges to overcome before we can truly consider every child to be one of the 'team' in early years and childcare. The rationale for doing so has already been discussed in this chapter, but the child's voice can easily be lost in the day-to-day communications between team members and as such it is the practitioner's willingness and ability to tune in to children in the first place that are essential. The EYFS with its clear guidance on effective practice will play a key role in ensuring that every child's learning journey is based on their individual interests and experiences, but practitioners must be careful not to make assumptions about what those interests might be. It is only when they take time to reflect upon their own practice and consider how they discover what children's interests and needs are that they can be certain of meeting them.

Babies and young children all have their own unique ways of communicating their needs to adults. Mathivet and Francis remind us that 'the development of language and communication skills is much more than a technical achievement or a checkpoint on a developmental chart. It is an essential aspect of being human, of connecting to others, of sharing thoughts and ideas and, above all, being a member of a family, social group and wider community' (2007: 9), which is why it is so important for the practitioner to recognize all opportunities to really listen to the child's voice.

Picture of Practice

Jack and Lily (2 1/2 years old) are playing with wooden bricks in the home corner. They have spent several minutes moving bricks from a table at the opposite end of the room, where several of the children are playing. Lily is loading some bricks into the toy washing machine and Jack is using a brick to 'iron' a doll's dress. A member of staff approaches and tells them that bricks do not belong in the home corner and that they must take them back to the designated table. Jack wanders off to another activity and Lily tries to follow. Both children are bought back to the home corner and are supervised as they put the bricks back.

What are Jack and Lily telling us about how they want to play?

This example raises several points for reflection: is it wrong for Jack and Lily to want to move the bricks? Does it really matter if they are playing with them in the home corner? It might be that Lily who has been quiet for several days now needs to play away from her peers. It could also be argued that the activity was not sited suitably in the first place. The practitioner in this example does not appear to be listening or responding to the non-verbal communication that is happening.

Jack and Lily offer an example of how opportunities can be missed on a day-to-day basis; but sometimes even when organized efforts are made to 'consult' with children, they do not achieve the desired outcomes in getting the child's perspective across. There are some good examples of consultation projects where children have been invited to design their ideal indoor or outdoor play space; provided with crayons, catalogues and blank sheets of paper, children are encouraged to let their imaginations run wild as they create their own fantasy world but can be disappointed when those tasked with its creation fail to deliver. Undoubtedly, some useful information can be drawn from such exercises, but children can be left feeling disempowered as adults mould their ideas into an acceptable or achievable format.

One of the most important and successful consultation exercises involving children and young people informed *Every Child Matters* (DfES, 2004a) and provided the five outcomes mentioned earlier in the chapter; demonstrating that consultation can be a valuable tool. The message conveyed here is that while opportunities for listening to children can be contrived and planned for, it is the day-to-day experiences and an ethos of teamwork as defined in this chapter that can offer a starting point for anyone working with children and families.

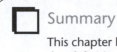 Summary

This chapter has offered an alternative model of the team by expanding the definition to include children and parents, and has offered some ideas about the way in which group dynamics and emotional literacy can impact upon team members. The reader is encouraged to consider their own practice and their position within the team, using emotional intelligence to understand the needs of others within the group. The introduction of the Early Years Foundation Stage (DfES, 2007a) offers further opportunities to reflect upon practice with themes and principles that further support the idea of inclusive teamwork in its broadest sense.

Personal and Professional Development Activity

The underpinning theme in both Chapters 3 and 5 is that of 'emotional literacy' and it is not difficult to extend general reading on this topic using the references provided. However, for the purposes of this chapter – and the emphasis on self-awareness in the text as a whole – a brief exploration of the notion that leadership involves providing for mutual support and meeting needs within a team will be timely, before progressing to the final section of the book. How comfortable are you with this idea? Had you thought previously about the challenges presented by meeting what will inevitably be some conflicting needs? Do you feel strong enough in yourself to take on a role as the leader that involves enabling, supporting and promoting the open and honest communications and relationships that this entails? It is possible to start small in reflecting on this.

Firstly, it may be useful to think in terms of the needs of the group and the 'stage' your team may have reached in terms of the life-cycle of groups – a lot of staff changes or changes in practice requirements will undermine achievement of team goals, for example. This approach will also help to assess the 'bigger picture' in terms of the ability of the team and individuals in it to 'perform', removing the focus on dynamics between individuals and de-personalizing areas of tension.

Having reflected on this, it is then possible to consider the needs of individuals within the practitioner group. For example:

- What do you understand by the 'needs' of individuals in the team?

- How are these needs met in the team?

- What are your own needs?

- How are your needs met in the team?

- What do you do to support the needs of individuals in the team?

- In what ways do individual team members support your needs?

- How does your practice enable you to be confident that children's voices are 'heard'?

- Does pedagogic practice include the recognition, naming and acknowledgement of emotions for all – or just the conscious support for children's development?

This reflective model can be applied to all who fall within the broader concept of the 'team' and can also offer solutions to the types of conflict demonstrated in the pictures of practice above. It also suggests a structured framework with which to develop from 'managing with the heart' (Goleman, 1996), towards strategies for emotionally intelligent leadership.

Suggested Further Reading

de Board, R. (1998) *Counselling for Toads: A Psychological Adventure*. East Sussex: Bruner-Routledge.

Here, Toad learns how to analyse his own feelings and develop his emotional intelligence. It is a great 'sequel' to the original *Wind in the Willows* and a useful introduction to features of psychology, counselling and positive relationships.

Goleman, D. (1996) *Emotional Intelligence: Why Can it Matter More Than IQ?* London: Bloomsbury.

This is essential reading for anyone who wants to gain an understanding of emotion and rationality for self-awareness, and in order to understand the emotional needs of others.

Maslow, A.H. (1998) *Maslow on Management*. New York: Wiley and Sons.

This text develops insight into Maslow's influential theories of self-actualization and relates it to the motivation of adults in the workplace.

Siraj-Blatchford, I., Clarke, K. and Needham, M. (eds) (2007) *The Team Around the Child – Multi-agency Working in the Early Years*. London: Trentham Books.

This book is firmly grounded in practice and addresses some key issues for both policy makers and practitioners.

6

Mentoring and Supporting Teams

Alison Robins and Sue Callan

Chapter Overview

This chapter explores the notion of mentoring to consider why and how the skills used by a mentor are an important part of support within teams: for inspirational leadership, in the management of change and as an essential element of working effectively with children and their families. It considers the potential challenges inherent within mentoring relationships and gives practical suggestions, drawn from examples of effective practice, for the use of a mentoring system within settings.

Mentoring

Mentoring has been talked about for a number of years but, surprisingly, very little was published in this area until the 1990s (Parsloe & Wray, 2000). Even today, the majority of texts focus upon mentoring within the business or educational field, yet the skills and benefits involved can be considered to be universal across teamworking environments. *Mentoring in the Early Years* (Robins, 2006) was written as the result of a perceived need to 'fill a gap' in published material which relates specifically to the early years sector. The text aimed to serve the diverse 'types' of mentoring within early years settings. For the purposes of this chapter, we are suggesting that mentoring in practice is largely about identifying, and then nurturing, the potential within an individual in a way that enables them to set and own their goals. As part of this process, it is important for that individual to have ownership of the mentoring process while being supported in their personal and professional development. If we consider the key themes from the Early Years Foundation Stage (EYFS) (DfES, 2007a), and the principles which underpin these, it could be argued that 'mentoring' is indeed happening in practice as we nurture the children in our settings, for example, in the promotion of positive behaviour.

To link these themes to the working practice of leaders and practitioners within early years settings, the wording can be altered by leaders and reflected upon in relation to support for other practitioners. The themes are underpinned by principles that guide practice, and effective mentoring can therefore be part of value-based leadership, the outcomes of which are explored in Chapters 1 and 2.

 Point for Reflection

Unique practitioners

Every practitioner is a competent learner who can be resilient, capable, confident and self-assured.

Positive relationships

Practitioners learn to be strong and independent from a base of supportive secure relationships with colleagues or a key person.

Enabling environments

The environment plays a key role in supporting and extending practitioners' development and learning.

Learning and development

Practitioners develop and learn in different ways and at different rates and all areas of learning and development are equally important and interconnected.

These altered statements relate clearly to the focus of this chapter and it could be argued that they will be applicable across the board from newly appointed or newly qualified practitioners to experienced managers and leaders. Mentoring, like learning, is lifelong and, at its most effective, one will support the other.

Mentoring in Context

In 2005, the DfES published a document that focused on the *Key Elements of Effective Practice* (KEEP) (DfES, 2005c). This offered guidance to local authorities in their work with providers of government-funded early education. Although the audience was fairly narrow, the messages within this document can be applied across all providers within the sector whether they are maintained, private, voluntary or independent. The guidance stated that:

> Effective practice in the early years requires committed, enthusiastic and reflective practitioners with a breadth and depth of knowledge, skills and understanding. Effective practitioners use their own learning to improve their work with young children and their families in ways which are sensitive, positive and non-judgmental. (DfES, 2005c: 3)

Support from colleagues in order for practitioners to achieve all of these is essential and the role of a mentor is crucial.

The support a mentor provides should enable practitioners to reflect upon, monitor and constantly strive to maintain and improve their practice. This has inextricable links to the provision of quality care and provision within early years settings. Leaders and managers have a responsibility to provide high quality care and education, judged primarily by the inspections they undergo (Ofsted, 2006). These inspections will ask 'what is it like for a child here?' and the judgements made will be based upon the outcomes for children that are set out in law (DfES, 2004d) and also reflected in the statutory requirements within the EYFS (DfES, 2007a).

Leaders and managers in early years settings will be mindful of these standards and the quality of provision expected and will use the EYFS and Ofsted guides to support them in the development and maintenance of this quality. Standards also relate to expectations of people themselves. An increasing number of Children's Centre leaders have undertaken the National Professional Qualification in Integrated Centre Leadership (NPQICL), which has at its heart a set of standards relating to the 'knowledge, professional qualities and skills expected of those leading such complex, multi-disciplinary teams and organisations' (NCSL, 2007: online). These standards set out a 'recognised quality for professional best practice [with the aim of] introducing consistency for children and families across the country as well as recognising the important role these leaders play'. The standards focus on six key areas, with two of these relating to encouraging enthusiasm for learning among families and staff and forging strong working relationships with all related parties. 'Part of the "quality" within early years settings is to be found in the inter-actions between settings, practitioners, the children and their fami-lies' (Fowler & Robins, 2006: 43) and effective mentoring will play a crucial role in these relationships. An example of this in practice is illustrated below.

Picture of Practice

The following comments were made by a Children's Centre leader.

The centre has created a learning environment where everyone, including parents, mentor each other by learning together, learning from each other and learning through trial and error. This is some-thing that can be achieved when relationships are trusting and strong. As a centre leader, I am not the expert in everything and it is the team that provides expertise in all areas collectively. The team is strong because of:

- quality relationships
- effective communication
- drawing on each other's strengths.

As a result, the centre has developed an 'ethos' that everyone is equal and able to make a valuable contribution. We learn together how to get the very best out of each other.

The concepts of Reggio Emilia have enabled us to look at following the child's lead and developing their learning with them as co-researchers, building on existing strengths and interests. These concepts and actions are also applied to the adults, whether staff or parents.

Confidence can be an issue and a major barrier to involvement. Some people perceive that they have nothing to offer but through mentoring and support can offer a great deal. Mentoring is essential to get the very best out of staff and parents and can be achieved in many different ways, so we need to be creative as professionals about how, where and when this takes place – for example, in my experience, the most effective mentoring for parents is often done informally in groups or conversations rather than more formal approaches. Once we have mastered this, we may then have services that truly deliver support that makes an impact as it will be needs-led as opposed to service-led.

Over recent years, the Children's Workforce Development Council (CWDC) and its partners have recognized that while 'there is a great deal of high quality early years practice led by highly skilled practitioners [there is an ongoing need to] increase levels of training and development across the early years workforce' (CWDC, 2006: 3). Consequently, the introduction of the EYFS includes provision of training for Early Years Professional Status (EYPS). The key aims of this training are to set the minimum standards required by professionals charged to lead the EYFS, raise the quality of provision and support practitioners as agents of change within early years settings. This training, as with the NPQICL, is underpinned by a set of standards which reflect the need of the Early Years Professional (EYP) to be able to lead and support others.

It is clear that a significant part of the quality within settings relates to the people working within them and also their practice. In order to ensure quality, settings need 'committed, enthusiastic and reflective practitioners with a breadth and depth of knowledge, skills and understanding' (DfES, 2005c: 3). These attributes apply to everyone working within a setting, not just the practitioners who have undergone NPQICL or EYPS training, and the challenge for leaders and managers is the nurturing of these attributes in their staff, and also in themselves. Nurturing these attributes through self-awareness is considered in Chapter 2.

The skills and approaches associated with mentoring nurture and encourage these attributes in all practitioners but mentoring needs to be thought through and planned in order to be fully effective. Aubrey (2007: 84) supports this by noting that 'planning, designing and implementing an effective mentoring system for leaders and their learning communities is essential'.

The Approach to Mentoring

Within early years settings, mentoring may occur between adults and children, between children and children, adults within the settings and adults within a wider context including other practitioners and settings, parents, families and the community. Mentoring can range from very informal chats over coffee to a more formalized and structured system of arranged, monitored and recorded meetings. The purpose may be to share and discuss a personal or professional issue, in confidence, in order to find a way forward, or it may be mentoring as part

Mentoring approaches provide a framework of support within the adventure playground of learning and development

of a programme of study with the aim of discussing approaches to practice, setting targets and recording and monitoring progress.

 Pause for Thought

> Reflect upon the description of mentoring as identifying and nurturing the potential within an individual in a way that enables them to set their own goals. Begin to list the different types of 'mentoring' relationships that may exist within your setting.

Mentoring should be seen as a 'dynamic system of advice and support in the context of ongoing professional training and personal development' (Callan, 2006: 10) and is undertaken in a way that seeks to empower others. Even chats over coffee can be seen in these terms, but when it is recognized that relationships between individuals are based upon a mentoring approach, decisions need to be made about how formalized these need to be – a feature also discussed by Callan (2006) in terms of various mentoring styles and strategies.

It is extremely difficult, if not impossible, to provide a 'one size fits all' approach to the consideration and development of a mentoring system since much depends on the size of the setting and the staff available to act as mentors. Childminders, for example, might often work alone within the home environment. Mentoring support for childminders may come through visits from a local authority mentor teacher (a formal system), or (informal) daily or weekly meetings with other childminders when they take children to the local toddler group, or from more formally established local childminder forums and networks. Larger settings, such as a primary school, also receive support from a visiting mentor teacher and will have individualized mentoring in place for new colleagues or those undertaking a new role. Mentoring could also take place on a group basis when there is a shortage of mentors or where some people are unwilling or unable to fulfil the role for whatever reason. 'The dynamics of dialogue within a group are manifestly and significantly different from those in a one-to-one relationship' (Clutterbuck, 2005: 1).

Group mentoring has its losses as well as its benefits.

Benefits of Group Mentoring

• Discussion and sharing of multiple perspectives on an issue.

• A sense of shared concerns and mutual support (if the process is managed well).

• An opportunity for the setting to identify common issues (Clutterbuck, 2005: 1).

Losses of Group Mentoring

• The sense of total concentration on the individual – this is a key factor in establishing and maintaining rapport and trust.

• Time to reflect – in a one-to-one relationship, it is easier to have periods of quiet thinking space.

• Confidentiality – it is hard to be fully open, especially about emotions, in a group.

Given that mentoring can and will take many forms, there are certain things that will need to be considered in order to identify the best approach, given the context of the setting. Creative thinking may be needed and planning and adjustments will be essential along the way for any system to be successful.

Practicalities of Mentoring

Mentoring in practice, as mentioned earlier, is about identifying and then nurturing the potential within an individual in a way that enables them to set and own their personal goals. It is important for that individual to have ownership of the mentoring process while being supported in their personal and professional development.

As a starting point, it is important to consider what you, your setting, your colleagues, the children and their families might gain from using a mentoring approach. This will be different according to the size and type of setting but it is important to find a way of discussing possibilities so that any plans are then agreed, understood and owned by everyone. The facilitator of these discussions, who could be the setting leader, needs to take a motivational approach and hold a vision of collegiate support, improvement and progress with the recognition that all dimensions of change result from reflective practice and take time.

An understanding of what support through mentoring entails is important. Clutterbuck (2004) suggests that human instinct leads us to pass on information, knowledge and wisdom to others and it may be that many of us see this as the role of a mentor. He then provides us with somewhat of a warning:

> It often occurs that the desire of the more experienced person (especially if he or she is much older) to pass on accumulated wisdom exceeds greatly the desire of the less experienced person to listen. Most people may have the instinct to be a mentor, but to do the role well requires a capacity to hold back and allow people to learn for themselves. (Clutterbuck, 2004: 3)

Once the reasons for, and benefits of, a mentoring approach are understood and agreed as a way forward, there are certain things to be taken into account that apply universally to all situations. These could be discussed as part of professional development within a setting including all parties involved, whether this then involves mentoring occurring between colleagues, between practitioners and children or between practitioners and families. The following issues are discussed more widely in Callan (2006) and Callan and Copp (2006).

Credibility – Credibility is essential to the ability to mediate between the various parties involved in a mentoring relationship. A mentor must strive to establish credibility with everyone involved in the process in order to effectively support learning and reflective practice.

Clarity – Anyone acting in a mentoring capacity needs to ensure that the arrangements put in place between themselves and a mentee are, where necessary, negotiated with the leader of a setting in order to achieve clarity of their role and the purpose of the relationship.

Confidentiality – Mentoring will invariably take place within an ethical framework of good practice where confidentiality is paramount.

Time – in any busy setting, time is always a resource that is stretched. Mentoring requires time to meet, share and discuss and the challenge for practitioners, leaders and managers is to facilitate this. Creative thinking is often called for as well as forward planning.

Picture of Practice

Amanda works as a Children's Centre teacher part time and also with the school adjacent to the Children's Centre, in her capacity as a local authority mentor teacher. Her two roles complement and enhance each other as well as strengthening the links between the two settings. She has been able to facilitate weekly meetings between the school and the centre and make suggestions to the school regarding 'good practice' she sees in the centre. Sam, the nursery manager for the nursery based in the Children's Centre, has been supported by Amanda as her mentor. Amanda has arranged for Sam to visit the school to discuss areas of practice, while recommending to staff at other settings she visits that they visit the centre to observe and discuss practice. This is a good example of **cross-setting mentoring**.

Sam recognizes how Amanda has mentored her and their relationship is now one of mutual support. She acknowledges the part Amanda has played in encouraging her to become a mentor to others. Within her nursery manager role, Sam believes that she often mentors colleagues without them knowing. Simply posing the right questions in the right way can have an impact on

(Continued)

(Continued)

others, their thinking and their practice. Saying things like, 'do you know, I tried this approach last week and it really seemed to work – what do you think?' Often this will encourage the person she is talking to to try things for themselves!

The relationship between Amanda and Sam has developed over time. Sam said that they are very similar in their beliefs and approaches and that the relationship is easy. She believes that really successful mentoring is based upon good relationships.

Leaders as Mentors

When we consider the mentoring role from the perspective of a leader and manager, it may be argued that from this position, certain elements of the process may fall within their domain (such as organization of time management to facilitate mentoring contact in the team). However, it might also be considered that, at times, when the role of the leader and manager includes, for example, a responsibility for conditions of service, pay and performance of staff members, acting as a mentor may not sit easily with these (Aubrey, 2007). Leaders should recognize this distinct role of mentor, rather than the 'authority-figure' aspect of the management role. For instance, an effective mentor will never ask, 'how can I make (this person) change?' and will accept that colleagues will ultimately make their own choices about taking the risks inherent in personal development. Considered from a different perspective, it may also be the case that an effective mentor, whether or not a leader and manager, will facilitate reflection and professional development for their colleagues or 'mentees', and it is perhaps the responsibility of the leader to identify the most honest and effective approach to establishing mentoring in the team. We might also question whether or not the mentoring system and role is one which is perhaps shared between various people and in fact includes children and parents too – an aspect which is explored in the picture of practice below.

 Pause for Thought

How do you recognize who the right person is to mentor a colleague? Can this role be shared and, if so, how?

It is important for leaders and managers to question and reflect upon their role as a mentor within their team and this will undoubtedly have links with their style of and approach to management. For example, some managers will prioritize their mentoring in terms of a coaching role (Callan, 2006), transmitting information, modelling and support for skill-based job functions which might later be assessed formally in the workplace. This coaching will encourage, equip and enable others to increase their skills and be relatively short-term in duration, perhaps related to induction periods. In this scenario, other staff may well be asked to offer emotional/relational mentoring in the longer term based on colleagues' responses to experience in the job role.

Picture of Practice

This 'picture of practice' comes from the manager of a rural setting which operates on two sites.

> As overall manager, I have responsibility for sustaining and improving standards and practice and delegating administration tasks.
>
> When considering who may be the right person to be a mentor, I believe it depends on the type of setting and also the type of mentee as to whether a manager is the right person. In my setting, I have two co-managers who work alongside me and we share issues associated with the management role – including problem solving. As far as our role as mentors goes, it depends on the mentee's character and also the combination of staff and children they are working with in a session.
>
> If the manager is hands-on and the mentee is on their shift and also has a good relationship with the manager, then there is no reason why their mentor should not be the manager. However, recently we have been supporting a very timid student who is young and obviously sees the managers as 'authority' to be feared. This has been revealed through her whole body language and expression so we made the decision to pair her up with Sam who is fun-loving and completely wacky and Tom, with whom she frequently works. This way, she is getting the support she needs and they are able to give this to her in a way that she responds to.
>
> If I reflect on myself as a mentor, I find that I can be too technical and go into much too much depth for people, so to overcome this

(Continued)

(Continued)

Lucy (one of my co-managers) will mentor me by suggesting how I might manage and deliver the support I am giving. I don't think mentoring is about levels of seniority – well, it isn't for me – it's about which person fits which person. I feel that just like children have schemas, so do adults in the way they approach things and the way they access information, and in order to support their development the same care needs to be taken over matching 'activity' and mentor to mentee. Just because I may not be mentoring, I wouldn't consider myself a failure. As manager, I would still be involved through the other mentors by checking in with them and discussing options.

To mentor effectively, I believe you enter into a shared process of mutual trust and a kind of dependency without being dependent. For managers with a more autocratic style, this must be an impossible concept.

All the strands of leadership and management discussed in this text require a leader who can negotiate the two aspects of professional practice: dealing with and organizing *systems* in tandem with developing and extending relationships involving *people*. This approach features in professional standards and in the recommended self-assessment activities contained in Moyles (2007), toolkits for working effectively with hard-to-reach groups (Together for Children, 2008) and quality assurance schemes.

Mentoring and Leadership

Leading and managing early years settings has become increasingly challenging with the plethora of changes and developments that have occurred, and will continue to occur within the sector. As indicated in the introduction to this text, 'many people … without any formal training or qualifications, have found themselves in a leadership and management role in increasingly complex small early years businesses and settings' (Moyles, 2006: Introduction). We are provided with the example of 'the playgroup leader, a mother of young children, who suddenly found herself responsible for, among other things … ensuring staff within the setting received opportunities for professional development' (Moyles, 2006: Introduction). It is to be hoped that all leaders and managers will now recognize the importance of emotional literacy and empowering relationships in teams. Certainly, we hope to have shown that part of this support can come through the experience of an empowering mentoring relationship (or relationships).

 Point for Reflection for Leaders and Managers

In your experience, where has mentoring support been found?

- colleagues
- training courses
- colleagues from cluster groups
- visiting mentor teachers
- a mix of informal/formal mechanisms

 **Activity**

Identify and add your own 'supporters'.

In Chapter 2, practitioner voices demonstrate that team members tend to look to their leaders and managers to inspire and guide them. This requires key characteristics to be inherent within the leader, and authors such as Rodd (2006) debate what these might be. The conclusion is that they relate to a person who considers lifelong learning important, as well as features of:

- curiosity (an interest in learning)

- honesty (principles and actions being open to public scrutiny)

- courtesy (treating others with respect and dignity)

- courage (a willingness to take risks, make mistakes and learn from them)

- compassion (creating trust, empathy, high expectations, hope and inspiration and providing opportunities for individual, group, personal and professional development) (Rodd, 2006: 37).

Pause for Thought

Is it the case that all leaders may consider themselves in terms of these 'warm' characteristics as part of working with children? Does the management of systems and leadership require a different emphasis of attributes and characteristics to avoid excessive pressure on the self?

All of these characteristics are personal attributes and some can be related to those needed in order to act as an effective mentor for colleagues, in particular, courtesy and compassion. Claxton (cited in Rodd, 2006: 37) considers that these characteristics are fundamental to leaders who are responsible for enabling, encouraging and evaluating other people: 'effective leaders need to be better learners so that they can help others to learn more effectively' (Rodd, 2006: 37). One of the standards for EYPS (CWDC, 2006: 8) states that those awarded this status 'must demonstrate through their practice that a secure knowledge and understanding … underpins their own practice and informs their leadership of others'. With these attributes, leaders and managers are able to become the instigators, encouragers and even role models for the mentoring process.

Change is one of the most inevitable things in life and management of change is discussed in Chapter 3. Most of us are very resistant to change and will go out of our way to avoid it. The recent climate and pace of change within the early years sector has no doubt left a significant number of practitioners feeling that they need a period of calm and stability. However, as Rodd suggests, 'much uncertainty and unpredictability still exists for practitioners as the profession attempts to accommodate rapid social change and develop services and programmes that are adaptable, flexible and responsive to community needs' (2006: 182). In order for the sector to grow and develop, change is necessary, and while managers and leaders will be fully aware of this, there is a need for them to have an understanding not only of the current climate, policies and directives but also of how change can be managed effectively. Effective mentoring plays a key part in this and, if planned carefully, can help managers and leaders achieve the necessary changes. Some people will see change as a threat to their values and beliefs, a threat to their position perhaps, perhaps a threat to the profession and an unnecessary waste of time, effort and resources that should be avoided. Others, however, will see change as exciting, a challenge, and will see the future benefits to themselves, their setting and to the profession.

Mentoring for Managers and Leaders

Leaders and managers are faced daily with managing change and being in this position is often described as being quite lonely. What is apparent from those practitioners featured in Aubrey's research (2007) is that the leader will need a professional critical friend or mentor in order to support them in their role.

 Point for Reflection

> Who does the person 'at the top' turn to for support and advice? By turning to and 'offloading' to fellow colleagues, does this undermine some relationships and the fact that, as leader or manager, much of the decision-making and resulting consequences rest with them?

Another question to consider may be the sort of relationship that a manager or leader develops with fellow colleagues.

The following thoughts come from the reflections made by a manager on the relationships they created with fellow colleagues and the importance of getting the balance right. It may be useful to question whether or not this approach is an inherent part of effective mentoring and also whether the same comments apply to our relationships with children.

- Always be firm but fair.

- Avoid obvious favouritism.

- Show an interest in people beyond their job.

- Try to keep a finite distance between you and the staff you are leading or managing so that they realize and can accept that you are 'the boss' and that they may have to sometimes accept your judgement in decision-making even if they disagree.

- Try to ensure your staff know that you will be honest and fair in decisions you make and will support them with decisions they make.

- In times when difficult decisions have been needed, never be afraid to admit later if they were wrong.

- Try to lead people to believe that when outcomes are good, although you may believe it was largely down to you, it was largely down to them. This can deliver big pluses.

- Do not try to solve inter-staff problems on the spot. Most will dilute and dissipate if left for a while.

- Enjoy the rewards and challenges of successful leadership and management.

There are some sound principles here but keeping a distance from colleagues will no doubt be against the instinct of many leaders and managers in early years settings because, as discussed above, we are in an environment that is one of nurturing and care. Consider the distress and difficulties that may occur if issues are brought to the attention of the managers by parents or staff members that need dealing with where an employee is at fault. These obviously need to be dealt with in an appropriate manner and this could be tricky where relationships are too close. Aubrey (2007) refers to one of the leaders in her study as noting that the position of a manager is indeed lonely and in fact this 'places leaders in isolation and often in an authority position in respect of friends' (2007: 84). Leading and managing can be a lonely business and it is important to consider how leaders and managers are mentored and supported while working to develop and inspire teams.

Support can often be gained by leaders and managers mentoring each other on a 'cross-setting' basis, as mentioned earlier, and the development of cluster groups of settings may provide a network where staff training may also be shared and opportunities are taken to discuss practice. Learning from experience is something that we hold very strongly within the sector as one of the principles associated with the learning and development of young children. Even when they get things wrong, we facilitate children's learning through these experiences and allow them to move forward. When someone finds themselves in a leadership or management position, there can be a danger that they feel they should have all the answers and should not be seen to fail. Perhaps colleagues also hold this view and consider that if a person has reached this level within their career, they can provide exactly what is needed to consistently support and lead a team and that the leader does not have a need for outside support. In an earlier picture of practice, the manager alludes to having colleagues to turn to for support who act as mentors. If mentors need to be suitably 'matched' to their mentees, how is this achieved when the support that is needed may not be found 'within house'? Networking can provide such opportunities but the networking itself needs to be thought about and created. If this appears problematic, a starting point may be simply asking an 'outside' colleague if they will act as a mentor. Aubrey (2007: 84) suggests that 'long-term support systems and relationships among early childhood leaders are essential'.

Pause for Thought

How can your own personal support networks be expanded or enhanced?

What are the opportunities for using both formal and informal networking processes in order to actively choose your 'supporters'?

Visiting Mentors

Outside mentors can bring something different to the quality and progress of a setting by sharing knowledge and experience, and being in a position to be able to consult with colleagues from their own 'workplace' and thus provide further multi-professional links. 'Outsiders' who come in to settings to provide support and training are often received differently from internal people. One particular trainer advertises his approach as being 'similar enough to be listened to but different enough to be heard' (Seel, 2007: online). Outside mentors can perhaps challenge in ways that close colleagues cannot. Providing a visiting mentor teacher carries credibility, has an ability to support that is based upon sound and current knowledge, and approaches the process in a way that develops two-way respect and trust – this type of relationship can provide rich rewards. A possible challenge with this type of mentoring is that the 'mentor' in this situation will not necessarily be freely chosen.

Reflective Activity

Reflecting upon what you have read so far, consider the benefits of the support received from a visiting mentor as opposed to a mentor who is 'within house'. Add to the bullet points below to collate your thoughts.

Benefits of a visiting mentor

- a fresh pair of eyes
- emotional detachment from the dynamics of the group

Benefits of an 'in-house' mentor

- knowledge of group culture
- ease of access to staff for spontaneous mentoring opportunities

Mentoring in Practice with Children and Families

Few practitioners would be able to say that they have never encountered a difficult situation when working with parents. However, where relationships are characterized by positive approaches and those involved know each other well, it is likely that in the longer term, the partnership will be sustained despite occasional tension. Practitioners need to be willing to reflect on their own reactions and responses to significant incidents in order to find ways to develop their skills in this area.

The qualities of the professional collaboration and mentoring described in the earlier picture of practice from a Children's Centre represents the firm foundations on which effective strategies for work in teams and with families can evolve. In the context of integrated provision, there are various 'layers' of mentoring apparent. There is professional mentoring across agencies represented by the centre teacher and nursery manager relationship, the centre leader and service agency collaboration and exchange, and the nursery manager/practitioner relationships that in turn inform the relationship with families accessing the centre itself. These layers can be extended if the themes discussed in Chapter 7 relating to parent involvement and mutual support groups are taken into account – ultimately, all practitioners can model and support opportunities for facilitating mentoring relationships *with* and *between* parents.

The use of mentoring techniques is most obvious in long-established voluntary sector organizations such as the Pre-school Learning Alliance (PLA) and National Childbirth Trust (NCT), but is increasingly developing in Children's Centres with breastfeeding support groups, dads groups (including social activities such as centre-based five-a-side football teams), Play and Talk and craft groups. It should be recognized that other practitioners not working in integrated centres will also be involved in mentoring relationships with parents as part of their professional role – health visitors, childminders, portage workers, family support and inclusion workers working as Special Educational Needs (SEN) play therapists are some particular examples. It is helpful to think of mentoring as a conscious strategy for developing practice for work with children and families. While parents may initially regard the practitioner as an 'expert' (thus accepting credibility in the role), this perception can evolve into that of a 'supportive friend' through use of the mentoring approaches and techniques. Once considered in these terms, it becomes apparent that positive relationships between all adults involved in supporting outcomes for children can be assessed in terms of 'quality' using mentoring principles. The following picture of practice illustrates this point and demonstrates the possibilities for mentoring in work with families.

Picture of Practice

Safeguarding children

A good example of multi-layered mentoring in action is the Home-Start organization – a nationally organized, voluntary sector body providing befriending and support for parents of children under five. Managed by local coordinators, community-based programmes recruit volunteers and coordinate training and development for those who will undertake home visiting. Parents needing help can self-refer, or may be recommended to do so by health visitors and other services. Support can be long or short term and the families decide whether to take advantage of what Home-Start can offer and when to terminate their 'contract' with the organization. This will be done through direct contact with the area organizer. What is most significant is that Home-Start volunteers are all people who are parents and have experienced the challenges of caring for young children. In this way, Home-Start empowers parents to share and use their own experience with others. The management of procedures for safeguarding children is most important in the context of an enabling environment for positive parenting decisions. If a volunteer reports concern about a child/family in this respect, then the local area coordinator may visit the family to encourage discussion of the situation and to support self-referral to child protection agencies, if this seems appropriate within statutory procedures (DfES, 2007e). However a referral is made, Home-Start will continue to support the family throughout this process. In the current context of practice where there are established limits to confidentiality and a requirement for agencies to share concern, this strategy of management keeps the family at the centre of positive practice while promoting outcomes for children.

This example demonstrates the layers of mentoring that become apparent when 'unpicking' the characteristic features of non-judgemental, respectful practice through positive relationships. It also suggests an example of a scenario where practitioners may themselves require the support of a mentor in dealing with their own responses to situations encountered as part of the job role. While this support might be found in the practice of supervision in teams, a mentoring relationship with a 'professional critical friend' will enable the practitioner to work through personal responses, some of which may be based on emotions that may be a barrier to the professional role in supporting a family. This may be particularly the case for those who regularly carry out home visits and whose effectiveness necessitates a more personal relationship and regular contact with the family.

The example also extends the themes of emotional literacy raised in Chapter 5, as does the area of work in supporting families of children with special needs. Parents in this situation have faced a major challenge to their self-confidence, and the level of professional 'intrusion' in their lives can lead to a loss of autonomy. Before they can take stock and think in terms of the potential of the child, parents have to work through powerful feelings and responses. These may involve conflict and tension among family members, social isolation or implications for their working lives and other children in the family. These experiences can initially place limits on partnerships and engagement in the 'processes' related to SEN provision.

At this point, practitioners commonly need to share with a mentor figure their frustrations resulting from feelings that the parents seem not to recognize the needs of the child. A mentor will help the practitioner to recognize that powerful feelings are a feature of the experience for both sides and find ways of recovering a professional approach in practice. In the longer term, some parents in this position go on to become effective mentors for others and make a considerable contribution to support networks and services.

Mentoring in teams can assist practitioners to work through some of the day-to-day challenges of maintaining positive approaches and attitudes to working with families. Chapter 7 includes consideration of practitioner responses to parenting styles and how this particular example can contribute to personal and professional development benefits for staff. It is certainly the case that work in the sector is emotionally and physically draining – working towards positive and inclusive practice across teams and involving families requires practitioners to 'give away' a great deal of personal energy. Mentoring is a means of returning and sharing positive energy with each other – think in terms of your personal energy as a reservoir that needs to be topped up if the supply is to be maintained!

Final Thoughts

Rather than 'summarize' this chapter, we would like to recognize the role of mentoring within the wider perspective of current practice and parenting goals. The chapter introduction was based on consideration of the themes of the EYFS and the five outcomes of ECM for children and young people. Arguments promoting the benefits of mentoring could point directly to practice with children and the way that they are 'mentored' by adults through their journey to 'maturity'. This journey was recently described by one father of adolescents as something like trying to land a reluctant fish, in that the line representing your relationship/ authority with the child needs to be gently handled or the fish is likely to be damaged and cannot be returned to the pool. Colleagues in key stage 3 work hard to support and mentor students to achieve their potential in this part of the learning journey and there is an increasing use of techniques such as reflective learning journals and peer mentoring within this. This directly replicates positive aspects of early years practice, where adults scaffold the youngest children in ways of establishing respectful and sensitive awareness of others, consultation and negotiation with children allowing for personal control over decision-making and choices at an age-appropriate level. Demonstrating positive relationships to children and young people through respectful work with their families and open communication in teams helps to enhance their involvement in social and cultural processes. Mentoring, in order to attain all that we are capable of, underpins the emotional literacy required by effectively functioning human beings and helps meet the need to achieve positive self-esteem and love and belonging in nurturing environments.

Personal and Professional Development Activity

While leaders may now be inspired to develop as mentors, it is important to recognize that, within the wider perspective, mentoring roles often include advocacy in terms of the needs, developing self-esteem and confidence of practitioners, children and families in the setting. To do this effectively, practitioners need a deep understanding of the context in which practice operates. Continued professional development is a means of acquiring this understanding and for taking responsibility to ensure that the workplace is represented and engaged in key issues and debates for change. This may include:

- pay and conditions and the status of the sector

- the experiences of communities, children and families

- participation in research and writing

- participation in consultation exercises as part of policy development processes. (This makes good business sense for one thing. Forewarned is forearmed!)

Suggested Further Reading

Clutterbuck, D. (2004) *Everyone Needs a Mentor: Fostering Talent in Your Organization* (4th edn). London: Chartered Institute of Personnel and Development.

This text is useful to leaders and managers who would like to be aware of the wider experience of mentoring in business and education. Clutterbuck Associates also has a very informative website – www.clutterbuckassociates.co.uk

Dahlberg, G., Moss, P. & Pence, A. (1999) *Beyond Quality in Early Childhood Education and Care: Postmodern Perspectives*. London: Routledge Farmer.

This is a useful text for developing awareness of wider contextual issues and debates for change/service provision.

Robins, A. (ed.) (2006) *Mentoring in the Early Years*. London: Sage.

This book is designed as a practical guide for anyone involved in the mentoring process.

7

Working with Families and Parent Groups

Sue Callan and Alison Morrall

Chapter Overview

This chapter considers the context, literature and professional principles underpinning work with parents. Our definition of 'parents' relates to the role described in law – mothers, fathers, carers and all those who have taken on this role in children's lives, either temporarily or as a biological family. Similarly, the term 'father' can include male carers and other father figures.

Pauses for thought and pictures of practice are featured throughout in order to enable a reflective approach to work in settings. This framework is used to examine aspects of work with parents that present a challenge to leaders in personal experience of their professional role and responsibilities. As a result, this chapter is a working case study with which to plan for professional development needs and improvement actions in teams.

The self-awareness of the leader is crucial to success in working with parents. We assume that practitioners are committed to working collaboratively with parents and thus focus particularly on strategies to examine personal values and service delivery in settings, ensuring that these are aligned with sector requirements detailed elsewhere in this text. Leaders may choose to use the activities in this chapter as a basis for conversation with a professional critical friend or mentor as part of reflective practice. Shared reflection and evaluation in teams also provides a means by which some aspects of practice can be distributed to colleagues, thus the strands of management discussed in previous chapters are significant to criteria for success in this respect.

Context

In this section, we present a brief overview of the wider context for practice. This is crucial to developing an understanding of the complexity of work with parents.

The statutory requirements and practice guidance (DfES, 2007a) for the Early Years Foundation Stage (EYFS) identify a clear responsibility for those leading and managing settings to place the child at the centre of practice. The importance and significance of work with the family to ensure continuity of experience and care for children is emphasized in the documentation as a recognized feature of quality provision and professionalism. In this respect, the setting is seen as an extension of the family in supporting the development and early learning of the child. Hence, working with parents is a feature of principled practice.

These principles are referenced in the documentation (DfES, 2004a) to the five outcomes for children in the Every Child Matters (ECM) framework and subsequent legislation, but are not new concepts. They can be identified in the work of early childhood pioneers in the United Kingdom such as Robert Owen, the McMillan sisters and Susan Isaacs, and continue in philosophies of practice around the world, notably in the Reggio Emilia schools (Italy) and the Te Whariki curriculum (New Zealand) mentioned in previous chapters. Such models are representative of the early years traditions, theory and philosophies underpinning the EYFS guidance (DfES, 2007a). However, applying the principles relating to partnership with parents might remain 'problematic' for some practitioners, despite the fact that many settings are able to engage with parents positively and benefit from the energy and enthusiasm that parents bring. Successful settings not only involve the family, but also work collaboratively with parents, at the same time fulfilling statutory responsibilities for curriculum delivery and safeguarding child welfare. It is this complex dynamic of responsibilities and relationships that result in challenges for professional practitioners across all agencies. If leaders and managers are to unravel this aspect of their role, it is imperative that personal professional development enables an awareness of the significance of external influences on day-to-day practice and the nature of 'partnership' with parents.

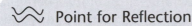 Point for Reflection

A newly appointed family support worker has recorded the follow-ing as part of a reflective conversation in the Foundation Degree in Early Years (December 2007).

Research on social policy has made me aware that I need to act as a 'voice' for families so I can raise awareness of issues affecting children and ensure they get support from politi-cians. Our work needs to be valued and continue to receive funding as part of this. I recognize that I must collaborate and support the multi-agency team that I encounter on a daily basis and that networking is vital in order to raise awareness of political issues and know who to lobby if I have concerns and want to implement change.

The advocacy role recognized here will not necessarily result in a culture of dependency between practitioner and parents if issues, attitudes and values explored in this chapter are part of this stu-dent's critical reflective practice on her role.

The relationship between parents and practitioners is part of the com-plex interrelationship of various cultural, social and political struc-tures and organizations. Practitioners will be aware that the roles attributed to leaders and managers of settings are indicative of debates on the nature of childhood, children and the family in society. These issues are represented in the work of Dahlberg et al. (1999) and Foley et al. (2001). Any assessment of values and principles for practice must first acknowledge the social and cultural roles attributed to set-tings – if only to present a confident appraisal of ethical practice. Dahlberg and Moss (2005) also critically examine ethics and the polit-ical context for practice in relation to the transformation model of service provision – the potential to change lives and communities.

The transformation model has developed over time, parallel to the evolution of welfare provision. As an approach to practice, the trans-formation model extends the consideration of 'models' proposed by Daly et al. (2004), who describe the characteristics of practice that result from underlying attitudes towards parents and families. It is useful to make these models explicit in order to allow for reflection and exploration about personal values, ideas about 'partnership' and how roles and context might influence this – all of which are explored in this chapter.

- The 'expert' model practitioner assumes a negative attitude towards the child's experience in the home and family. There is a focus on what the child is *unable* to do and what the family *fails* to provide. As a result, the practitioner takes control of decision-making and there is little opportunity or encouragement for parents and carers to become actively involved.

- The 'transplant' model practitioner recognizes a limited role for the family/parents. Some responsibilities are handed over and parents may be consulted but not positively enabled to contribute to the decision-making process. This results in 'distant' relationships where the practitioner is perceived as an authority figure. It could be argued that this is a 'default mode' if practice is not critical or consistently reflective.

- The 'consumer' model practitioner is conscious of the concept of 'stakeholder' interests and rights relating to the provision of service. There is recognition of shared interests with the family in supporting the child and of links to business and quality orientation to practice. Practice is founded on the principles of the Ball Report (Ball, 1994) which recognized that parents are the most important people in children's lives. There is consistent effort to engage with parents in order to enable their full participation and choices in terms of decisions concerning the child. However, this model can result in the presentation of parents as a homogenous group in government policy promoting 'parent rights', which itself leads to tension when constraints are applied by different policy/services/forms of provision.

 Pause for Thought

Critical reflection on personal attitudes involves a developing consciousness about values and assumptions. Leaders and managers may wish to reflect on whether their practice involves a misalignment of approaches and attitudes which may undermine positive relationships with parents. Early Years Professionals are required to demonstrate knowledge and application of an ethical approach to practice that draws on context, theory and literature in order to demonstrate a transformational approach in the role. The remainder of this chapter seeks to provide such a framework in order to facilitate critical reflective practice.

Mekki (2004) shows how, historically, the provision of services to families can be located in the gradual development of 'welfare states' in many North European countries. In the United Kingdom, this is conventionally understood to culminate in the social legislation of the late 1940s which established universal education, health services and public housing to promote the welfare of the nation following the war of 1939–1945. The aim at this time was to provide services to all as a feature of the strategy to promote social cohesion. Funded through taxation and National Insurance contributions from those participating in the labour market, such universal welfare services would provide a means of supporting those who may be in temporary need of social or economic support. Child welfare in particular was a key area of concern as families and communities had been badly affected by the war. Although based on principles of social justice and mass movements for social and cultural change, one outcome of this approach was the responsibility placed on services to intervene in the lives of those perceived to require additional support in meeting the needs of children. A key objective was that social intervention through health professionals and the provision of universal State nursery education would not only assist families to re-establish disrupted employment patterns but also act as a means to prevent children entering the 'looked after' system. Services were initially provided on a 'done for' rather than 'done with' basis for those who needed them and this has undermined subsequent attempts to promote the empowerment of service users. It could be argued that a 'deficit' approach to work with families was apparent from the outset of the welfare system, and that later decisions by successive governments undermining economic commitment to universal provision have meant that targeted services emerged. These are focused mainly for those 'in need' and often carry some social stigma.

Baldock et al. (2005) provide further information about the relationship between policy and practice. For our purposes, the emergence of two key areas for reflection are apparent. Firstly, the possibility of positive and equal relationships will be influenced by the social context in which families make use of provision. Secondly, different service contexts may generate varying ideas about the nature of 'partnership' and approaches to involving parents. A key tension here is the extent to which the State is responsible for and can exert influence on the personal realm of the family.

The rationale for work with parents is not simply to enhance children's development and learning during early childhood. Sure Start programmes are based on government policies promoting social intervention to overcome poverty, and in preventative work where children are perceived to be at risk of not achieving positively within the five outcomes of ECM (DfES, 2004a). Sure Start principles are based on an enabling model in which families are to be facilitated towards positive social outcomes. However, families experiencing difficulties with fulfilling the role and responsibilities of parenting, or who are perceived as needing individual support, may be immediately placed in a 'dependent' relationship with practitioners unless values and attitudes in practice are made explicit through continued reflection and awareness in teams.

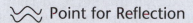 Point for Reflection

Understanding the concept of partnership

What do we mean by partnership? In this chapter, 'partnership' is characterized by a working relationship based on mutual respect, openness, democracy and sharing information or experiences, in order to promote equality and avoid discriminatory practice for children and families. It is recognized that there may be constraints in some roles or contexts to achieving this. Lead practitioners are encouraged to engage in reflection in order to determine the implications of this for their own setting and personal attitudes. The chapter also contains the opportunity to consider strategies to address those factors limiting parent engagement in partnership.

This concept of partnership has evolved over time and as the result of changing political ideologies, as well as shifting cultural and social attitudes to the family. As a result, the 'expert' model of provision and related attitudes started to break down once interpretations of partnership began to acknowledge the values explicit in the Ball Report (Ball, 1994) – that is, notions of the child's voice, parental rights, responsibilities and accountability – mixed with quality and consumer concepts in service delivery. Such values are reflected in contemporary service provision where institutional power remains for safeguarding responsibilities, while the Common Assessment Framework (CAF) requires collaborative working so that the 'team' also includes the positive engagement of parents (DfES, 2006b, 2006c). A criterion for success is that practitioner roles are carried out with a positive *attitude*, respect for parents and a willingness to engage as a supportive additional adult in carrying out the duties towards children described in legislation underpinned by ECM (DfES, 2004a).

Literature – the concept of partnership

The wider framework for welfare policy places great importance on parenting and family life (Langston, 2006), noting that the family unit is essential to the healthy early development and growth of young children. At the same time, there is recognition that the State benefits from supporting families in order to promote health, social order and cohesion for the national interest. Practitioners who wish to explore this sociological approach are directed to Foley et al. (2001).

For many families, use of early years services is a means of enabling participation in the workforce, promoting family economic security and achieving the healthy independence of its members. Those who also experience difficult personal and social/economic circumstances may require services to assist them with the demands of parenting. What unites these different experiences is the need for parents to feel accepted for their individual situation. This is clear in the parent perspectives outlined by Moss and Pence (1994). It is recognized that families require childcare for only a few years in their lives. That these are some of the most crucial years in terms of the developing child's growth and learning has been the driving force for both policy and practice – now extended by ECM (DfES, 2004c) – in outcomes for young people up to the age of 19.

Family structures and parent influences on children's psychology, development and learning are well documented. One feature significant to practitioners' understanding of their own interactions with parents is that of parenting 'styles' as discussed by MacLeod-Brudenell (2004). While parental style can be influenced by a number of factors, significant aspects include the characteristics of the individual child and the parent's sources of support. Bee (2000) discusses the resulting classification of parenting styles based on levels of parental responsiveness and warmth towards the child and expectations about the child's behaviour.

It is crucial that leaders recognize that such 'beliefs' also set the pattern of expectation that the parent will have *of* the setting, responses to experience *in* the setting and judgements made *about* the setting. This is the one area in which each parent and each family is genuinely unique. An overview of research for a range of parenting experiences and circumstances is also provided in Nutbrown (2006) and Quinton (2004).

As a result of this complex mix, leaders need to develop and maintain a clear vision for practice. Such clarity is characteristic of 'flagship' centres and has been a continuous feature of the work of Whalley (1994, 1997, 2001) in describing the development of the Pen Green Centre and its adult team. What is particularly evident is that such settings have managed to tread the tightrope of conflicting roles while developing positive relationships with parents who are in the most difficult personal circumstances. The strength of these teams has been the ability to recognize the role of practice in terms of the social welfare agenda while maintaining respect for individual rights and social justice (the concept of a team value bond is explored in Chapter 2). Positive practice does not lose sight of the fact that overwhelmingly families strive to do the best for themselves and their children. This attitude is the basis of positive relationships and will promote the well-being of parents, families and children as well as the success of settings. Parents and practitioners are mutually dependant and a constructive relationship will facilitate positive outcomes for children.

Undoubtedly, the playgroup movement has also been significant to an understanding of the positive benefits of partnership. Community pre-schools established a model for promoting parental control of settings through opportunity for direct involvement in management. McGivney's (2000) study for the Pre-School Learning Alliance (PLA) demonstrates that the PLA model of parent-led community pre-schools has been most effective in developing adult learning in local communities since the early 1960s.

The PLA model is one example of partnership working assessed in a number of texts that examine practitioner approaches to work with parents. These ideas result in the distinct 'models' of management culture and their impact on the possibilities for involvement, detailed in the opening section of this chapter. The true challenge for leaders in this respect is to understand and evaluate the context in which a service operates. This enables settings to develop effective organizational strategies for engaging in positive relationships with parents, whatever the limits placed on 'partnership' by the professional role.

The roles required of parents are varied. They include provision of resources, attending significant events, providing active assistance to planning and delivery of 'curriculum', positive collaboration in practice and (sometimes) control or management as with parent-run groups or school governorship. This is described as a participation continuum by Pugh and De'Ath (1989), which demonstrates that varied levels of personal investment are required of parents. Influenced by parenting styles, partnership can also be restricted as the result of negative self-confidence, aspects of family experience, feelings of exclusion – including barriers of language, culture and belief, restrictions of employment patterns or the previous unsatisfactory experience of practice.

Vincent (1996) proposes that this can offer ways of examining those features of practice that either do not enable parents to become involved or cause them to be unhappy with what is on offer. Overall, the shared characteristic of passive non-participation is lack of confidence and exclusion – intentional or otherwise. He contrasts this with non-participation where parents have made an active decision not to be involved because their overall perception of practice is positive. In any event, a willingness to critically reflect on our own values and practice will limit the likelihood of a 'them' and 'us' default mode and recognition of the responsibility to initiate change. The parent's right to information, consultation and partnership recognizes their role as advocate for the child in the setting, thus avoiding the perception that the world of the setting is a different culture to the child's experience of home and family.

 Pause for Thought

How could team leaders overcome inhibitors to parental involvement, such as:

- lack of confidence in literacy or communication skills
- letters not getting home
- overuse of jargon in letters and communication
- over formality in style of communication/event
- insufficient notice/times of meetings or events
- negative practitioner responses to parenting styles or family lifestyles?

How will you evaluate practice in order to initiate change and take account of a range of needs? Most importantly, how do you promote trust that the setting will be able to solve a problem for the parent/child?

While parents have personal reasons for non-participation, management of practice should continually take account of possible *needs* in order to ensure inclusive practice.

Tuning in to Practice

An effective leader/manager will ensure the organization of the environment plays a key role in supporting and extending parent and practitioner relationships, contributions to practice, personal development and confidence in their roles and responsibilities.

The remainder of this chapter will help clarify management and leadership priorities for work with parents. Hegarty (1993) explores this relationship as a dynamic process encompassing five aspects of practice from initial contact, induction, settling in, individual support, to readiness for transitions.

Pause for Thought

Building on established practice

- Can you identify the strategies currently employed in your setting to support the evolution of parent/practitioner relationships?
- Do you think that the idea of an *equal partnership* is realistic in all five areas? Is this feasible and/or realistic? Are you confident that the opportunity to be *fully involved* in each aspect is available to all parents in your setting?

The particular area of personal support to parents has been chosen for exploration in this chapter. With the EYFS (DfES, 2007a) themes and principles in mind, we focus on:

1 Positive relationships with unique parents

Every parent is a competent adult who is/can be resilient, capable, confident and self-assured. Parents can be facilitated to be strong partners from a base of open, consistent and respectful relationships with practitioners.

2 Promoting shared opportunities for adult learning and development

Parents gain their own outcomes from partnership with practitioners and these are examined as pictures of practice in this chapter. If we

Parent engagement provides a community of relationships to sustain learning and development

accept the concept of parents as co-partners in practice, then practitioners can also expect to learn from their involvement with families as part of reflective practice.

Positive Relationships with Unique Parents

Many commentators note that a common feature of family life – through pregnancy and during early childhood – is that the experience of parenting is a period of intense anxiety and can be challenging in terms of financial circumstances, difficult decisions about adult family roles and careers, and may require a negotiation of the cultural expectations of close family and community – and this is when things are going well! It is hardly surprising that the legal and guidance framework for assessment of children in need and their families allows for the concept of 'good enough' parenting (DOH et al., 2000; DfES, 2007e). Add into this dynamic, social isolation or exclusion – through the experience of lone parenting, a nomadic lifestyle, having a child with a disability or special educational needs, family health issues, post-natal depression, unemployment, or issues related to language and immigration – and the notion of parents having *personal* needs which a setting might help negotiate becomes immediately apparent. The first challenge for leaders is to establish a means of working with parents in order to get to know the unique features of each family, as the family experience will determine the expectations and requirements of and responses to the service offered.

Pause for Thought

Getting to know you

How could you engage current families in a review of your practice? Perhaps you meet children in their own homes – what are your strategies for getting to know the wider experience of the family? Are you aware of the work arising from Pen Green on changing materials and styles in order to engage fathers' interests and avoid gender bias? (Whalley, 2001).

For all these reasons, work with parents is recognized as 'challenging'. Often, this concept is extended to individual parents or to particular families and communities. Practitioners need to be wary of such value-judgements, which undermine positive relationships. Working with parents involves a recognition of difference and diversity in all definitions of the term as it relates to family structure, sexuality and gender issues, children in the 'looked after' system, language, disability and belief. Developing practice for all needs is to be based on a commitment to promote shared understanding in adult relationships while working within the law for ensuring the safety and security of children in the setting.

Pause for Thought

Promoting shared understanding about partnership in your setting

- What is my setting? What is our primary role in terms of social policy?

- What are the implications of this for practice with parents and partnership?
- Do members of my team share this recognition? Do parents? How can I check?

How will this review help you to solve potential challenges in relationships with parents?

Although all parents are service users, in some settings, parents are recognized primarily as service 'consumers'. They pay substantial fees for pre-school experience and daycare for their children and have high expectations of service providers and the professionalism of practitioners. This has lead to some creative approaches to meeting practical 'needs', with a few day nurseries coordinating local nappy, ironing and laundry services or providing a coffee bar and parents' lounge with a two-way mirror into the children's areas. Twenty-four hour provision, night and weekend services are also an emerging response to the needs of working parents' shift patterns. It is worth noting, however, that the matter of parenting styles cuts across many boundaries in the sector, just as family illness, problems of alcohol abuse, domestic violence and abuse or sudden bereavement are not limited to certain communities. Practitioners in settings can expect to use professional networks to give family support at any time.

Self-esteem and emotional literacy in teams is a feature of Chapter 5. The significance of self-image and self-esteem to adults' ability to engage in positive relationships should not be underestimated. In developing enabling environments, there is, inevitably, a focus on work with hard-to-reach parents or parents who are experiencing personal difficulties (Together for Children, 2008). These are the significant experiences that practitioners learn from as they seek to achieve inclusive practice. The focus is on adapting practice to facilitate positive partnership with parents, rather than on an expectation that parents must change in order to participate. Practitioners will gain professionally and personally from experience in this area.

The following examples from practice focus on developing ways to promote well-being and confidence in parents.

Parent and Child Groups (Stay and Play)

Many parents require help at certain times in their lives, whether it is coping with illness, a marriage breakdown, or the birth of a new child. In most cases, a relation or family friend gives this support. However, not everyone can draw on family or social scaffolding.

 Changing Lives Case Study – Empowering Barbara

Barbara, heavily pregnant with her third child, regularly attended parent/child interaction groups within a Children's Centre. She was observed to be struggling with managing the behaviour of her young family. The group facilitator diplomatically suggested that she may benefit from extra support and guidance through-out the latter months of her pregnancy. This was agreed and Barbara was helped to self-refer. A family support worker began regular visits to Barbara at home, suggesting strategies to help with her daily routines. This support continued after the baby was born, with great emphasis put on empowering Barbara. Twelve months later, Barbara is working voluntarily in a school and has completed a childcare course; she hopes to train as a teacher when her youngest child starts full-time school.

It is important in this case study that Barbara feels in control of her situation. One strategy employed helped Barbara identify the areas of her life where she needed support – see the feelings map shown in Figure 7.1. Using the plot lines given in the key, Barbara was able to consider aspects of her experience and highlight those causing most difficulty. Crucially, she was able to see that there were some areas in which she felt comfortable and supported. Discussion with the group facilitator enabled both of them to plan an approach based on long- and short-term priorities and needs. This strategy also enabled Barbara to recognize that she was able to work positively with family support and take a significant part in dealing with difficult issues.

Parents and Creative Groups

Creative groups are also a feature of collaborative work with parents. For example, family participation rotas or play events in daycare settings can be an opportunity for parents to develop their creativity.

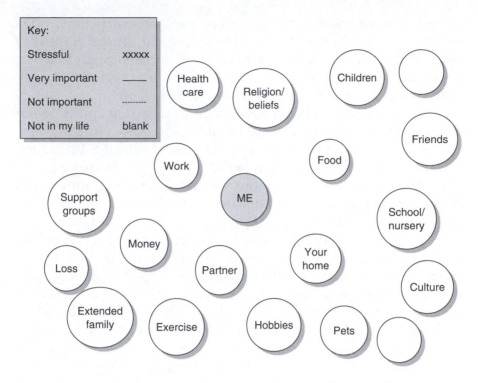

Figure 7.1   Feelings map (Morrall, 2008, adapted from Hartman, A., 1978)

One tiny voluntary sector playgroup in a rural area has developed an arts project as the direct result of adapting their curriculum to the Reggio Emilia approach. Supported by grants from the New Opportunities Fund, creative workshops run by a visiting artist are available for children, parents and other local practitioners. One vital outcome has been increased understanding and vocal support from parents for the playgroup's approach to the delivery of the Foundation Stage (DfES, 2000), and a cascade of contacts and shared approaches between local playgroups and schools.

What dynamics are at work in these examples? The rationale for creativity (including play) as part of working with parent groups is located in the ideas of humanist psychologists such as Maslow (1968) and Rogers (1983) and has been further described by the Pen Green team (Whalley, 2001). Fundamental to this are the concepts of individual potential and the significance of positive experiences and relationships to nurturing well-being and personal achievements. Being creative has the potential to provoke a multitude of emotions. Stephenson (2006) suggests that it can have a significant effect on a person's self-esteem and well-being. In addition, Rogers (2006) implies that emotions can impact on learning experiences, often affecting one's values and ability to understand. In the context of early childhood, it is important for early years practitioners to reflect upon the therapeutic value of art and crafts in enhancing parents' ability to show their emotions. Bruce (2006) suggests that creativity is part of every human being and it is up to early years practitioners and parents to pass this value on to young children. In effect, Burleson (2005) argues that the development of self-actualization and creativity within learning experiences could be described as one of the most important goals of our society. This belief is inherent in Reggio Emilia philosophy and practice and influences approaches to early learning across UK settings. In creative sessions, it is important that group facilitators take time to research and reflect upon the unique needs of each family when planning. Fowler and Robins (2006) stress that such reflection challenges thinking, enhances professional development and inevitably aids self-confidence, which is imperative for the role of group facilitator. Reflection is part of creativity and can be a positive outcome of such experiences for parents and practitioners. Often when new parents enter an existing group, the dynamics will change, therefore ongoing reflection and evaluation is required to keep a balanced, holistic approach.

Group facilitators should ensure that, irrespective of the group's main focus, a large proportion of time is dedicated to group discussion. Whalley (2001) notes that often parents find it hard to talk about themselves as people, seeing themselves 'only' as a parent. Miller and Devereux (2004) endorse this in recommending that parents are given a voice, and all contributions are welcomed in a non-judgemental forum. Getting in touch with one's feelings through dialogue with other group members is an extremely creative act; Rogers (2006) observes that it gives the contributor a confirmation of approval and acceptance within the group.

The fundamental aim of parent groups should be to enable and empower, thus boosting self-esteem. Group facilitation will recognize that positive comments can lead to a feeling of success and renewed effort. Quinton (2004) and Carlock (1999) suggest that high self-esteem makes life easier to cope with. It helps to deal with setbacks and disappointments, gives the confidence to take risks and leads to a feeling of empowerment.

It is important to note that for parents who have mental-health problems, this feeling of empowerment may be short-lived, as their self-esteem can fluctuate from one minute to the next. However, Goleman (1996) argues that short periods of high self-esteem are better than not experiencing a sense of self-worth at all. Social competency and healthy self-esteem go hand in hand; therefore, it is vital that parents are supported in addressing their stresses and mental-health needs in order to be a positive example for their children. Research by Miller and Devereux (2004) suggests that the collective experiences and support received by parents within parent groups can positively affect their decision-making concerning children's education. The emotional responses of staff to such a challenging area of practice must also be acknowledged and may be managed in some cases through the mentoring relationships discussed in Chapter 6.

Pause for Thought

All members of a team must be capable of contributing to positive relationships and supporting parenting. This will rely on the qualities of the leader. The importance of enthusiasm and passion for leading and developing practice will require recognition that this is one aspect of provision where *all* staff need to be *actively* involved. One criteria for success as a leader will be that all members of the team are facilitated to engage with parents in a way that represents professional principles – and are inspired to do so. What this represents is a management culture of high expectations for all those involved in service delivery and service use, and distributed responsibility for the management of practice.

With this in mind, how will you support those facilitators who may work directly with parents and families if your own role is less 'hands on' in a practical sense?

Leaders of early years settings who have contact with parents as part of their daily routine are an important catalyst for the development of positive relationships in multi-agency provision. When provision for children or the nature of the child's needs requires 'outside' contact, there may be barriers to forming relationships with those who are seen in positions of 'authority'. This may be particularly the case for some cultural groups – such as travelling communities – who feel that they have been subject to persistent discrimination and oppressive practice in the past. In any event, the self-confidence of the leader and the ability to facilitate this extended relationship can be an influencing factor in its success. Indeed, work with parents will inevitably lead to work with other professionals. This part of the team leader role is the means by which 'partnership' is transformed from the somewhat rarefied sphere of public policy into daily practice for children.

Fathers' Groups

There are several research papers concerning fathers' involvement in their children's early learning experiences. A report for the DfES (2003b) suggests that fathers are less able to develop a holistic understanding of their child's early experience and needs due to irregular attendance at group sessions. The report recommended that more consideration must be given to fathers' work schedules and economic role, money should be injected into working with fathers and that specific gender training should be offered to practitioners who facilitate these groups. Similarly, Goldman (2005) undertook specific research for the Basic Skills Agency into the relevance of fathers' groups, recommending that good practice would be to facilitate male-orientated, hands-on activities.

'I really treasure these sessions'

A father attending a craft session at a family contact centre revealed how much he valued the fortnightly visits spent with his children. He realized that he was missing so many of his children's learning experiences due to being an absent father, although he often thought about their development and learning needs. He reminisced a while about the pictures and painting his children had produced while under his supervision at the centre. Although admitting that prior to the family breakdown he had never thought about the value of 'sharing' the learning experience, experiencing these creative workshops alongside his children had opened his eyes to how much more they learn, socially, emotionally and creatively.

Recent research evidence indicates that children who spend quality time with their fathers are happier, find it easier to develop new friendships and are more likely to live honest and respectable lifestyles (Khan, 2005), implying further that these children often do better at school and in examinations. It is important at this stage to note that involving fathers in all types of family learning programmes will require high-level strategy, planning and commitment, and that a leader's role is to build a collective, positive ethos, among the whole workforce. Fathers benefit from spending time with other male carers in support groups and parent/child interaction groups (Whalley, 2001). In addition, fathers often gain firm friendships through these sessions, which can lead to a feeling of belonging, as noted above.

Crucially, it is in these situations that practitioners can come to an awareness of what partnership means for *parents*. This can be a very different perception from the expectations prescribed in the policy and practice framework originating from service planners. Most significantly, the leader will develop the means by which feedback from parents will be actively sought and recorded as part of a reflective practice cycle and improvement in the setting.

 ### Pause for Thought

How to seek feedback from parents

In terms of Ofsted inspection, work with parents is a feature for investigation, and practitioners might usefully self-assess by considering the question, 'what is it like for a *parent* in this setting?' Use of inspection reports, asking for feedback, suggestion boxes, and parent evenings are examples of formal opportunities for feedback.

- How could you record and make use of informal feedback such as the father's comment noted above?
- Are there opportunities for research (your professional development) in this respect?
- What are the internal criteria for success in judging parent perspectives of your practice?

Collaborative Participation and Adult Learning

The following instances of collaborative participation by parents demonstrate further the mutual benefits of partnership and allow us to conclude by highlighting adult learning possibilities. Leaders will aim for a model of practice where parents are actively involved in sustained activities to promote the child's development and learning. Sharing strategies such as observations, home–school links, reading and book groups, story sacks, play and talk, stay and play, photographic or video recording, schema spotting (as pioneered by the

Pen Green Centre) can all celebrate the child's experience and contribute to an awareness of diversity. In many settings, the need to include immigrant (newly-arrived) children who have a particular need of support in developing bilingualism has provided opportunities for parent and community volunteering and involvement. This has positively assisted inclusion in local communities and presented parents with a significant role in support of practitioners as well as opportunities for personal development.

Established support groups or parent-led pre-schools allow parents a higher profile in leading and organizing. This 'ownership' of a group enables personal skills development, and the opportunity to model positive parenting and social skills to those who are less confident. These present opportunities for all participants to gain further knowledge and understanding of early learning concepts by attending courses – often progressing through vocational training to higher education. Similarly, this participation in support of others offers parents the opportunity to engage in informal mentoring relationships – an aspect of practice discussed in Chapter 6.

Many parents provide activities and experiences which promote learning as part of family life at home. Some families and settings access resources and ideas on various internet sites, which will encourage the use of ICT by adults. But a challenge for partnership in this respect is that there is open communication from home into the setting, so that practitioners can also respond to the child's interests.

Recently, fathers' groups have become more popular, mainly held within schools, leisure centres or children's/family centres. In several counties, DADS advisors have been employed specifically by the Basic Skills Agency to offer practical advice and support on training and employment opportunities, signposting carers to other agencies where required. In addition, several specialist groups have been developed, specifically focusing on unemployed fathers where the main emphasis is put on gaining the skills for returning to work. Gaining the trust of fathers or any 'excluded' group takes time, but these groups deliver a variety of further learning opportunities, often tailored to the needs of the individual or focus group. Language and Play Awareness, Managing Family Finances and Basic Skills courses can often lead to further education courses or specific training, which in turn can lead to further employment opportunities. Most importantly, these groups allow fathers the time to socialize with others, share their experiences and form their own support network (www.dad.info).

Summary

In this respect, we have come 'full circle' because work with parents and facilitating parents' social networking depends on sound communication and relationships. Leadership will require an ability to manage the communications infrastructure that facilitates relationships with parents and organize the day-to-day work of the team delivering services to communities.

Personal and Professional Development Activity

Consideration should be given to the following dimensions for action, all of which have been featured in this book and included in this chapter:

- training and teamwork in the setting

- communication and positive attitudes to inclusive practice

- multi-professional contact and networking in integrated service provision.

These three dimensions form the basis of available self-assessment materials and resources accessible through organizations such as the National Children's Bureau (www.ncb.org.uk/PEAL). Settings can also address these issues through recognized quality assurance schemes.

Moyles (2007) offers leader-managers a self-assessment tool in the ELMS resources as does the Toolkit for Reaching Priority and Excluded Families (Together for Children, 2008).

Suggested Further Reading

For personal reading and investigation of policy and practice, the following are accessible introductory texts:

Baldock, P., Fitzgerald, D. & Kay, J. (2005) *Understanding Early Years Policy*. London: Paul Chapman.

Foley, P., Roche, K. & Tucker, S. (eds) (2001) *Children in Society*. London: Palgrave.

Whalley, M. (and the Pen Green Centre Team) (2007) *Involving Parents in their Children's Learning* (2nd edn). London: Paul Chapman.

Glossary of Terms

Advocacy
The active support of a cause on behalf of another.

Children's Centre(s)
Contexts within which children under five years old and their families can receive seamless integrated services and information, and where they can access help from multi-disciplinary teams of professionals.

Collegiate support
Support provided within teams where members are understood to have an equal standing.

CPD
Continuing Professional Development.

Critical friend
A trusted colleague who can provide support and comment in a constructively critical manner.

CWDC
Children's Workforce Development Council.

DCSF
Department for Children, Schools and Families.

ECM
Every Child Matters.

Emotional intelligence
Developing self-awareness and understanding of the impact our emotions have on ourselves and others.

Emotional literacy
The ability to perceive, understand and express feelings in a non-judgemental way, including skills for emotional control and awareness that enable relationships with others.

Extended Schools
Extended Schools work with the local authority, local providers and other schools to provide access to a range of integrated services.

EYFS	Early Years Foundation Stage.
EYPS	Early Years Professional Status.
Family	Any environment that provides facilities, continuity and nurture as the child progresses to maturity. There is no assumption that any particular way of constituting the family is of more value; we accept the notion proposed by Pugh and De'Ath (1989) that a family is simply what you find behind the door and that variation whether by chance or choice is now the norm.
Group dynamics	The forces and interactions that occur when people come together.
High self-monitoring	People who monitor and change their behaviour to fit different situations thinking that this is what people want to hear.
Home-Start	A charitable organization that provides support and advice to families of children under five.
Hot qualities	A range of skills needed to foster a proactive and visionary culture within a setting.
Inclusive practice	Inclusive practice is about participation, collaboration and including people: where individuals are fully involved in choices and decisions that affect their lives and in the matters that are important to them.
Inspirational leadership	A subjective perspective of interactions, intentions, emerging and established relationships and proactive responses to a variety of situations.
Leader/Manager	Those responsible for practice and the organization of services to support the children in their care.
Low self-monitoring	People who are consistent in their behaviour, thinking and actions across all types of interactions with other people.

Management of change	A structured approach to change in individuals, teams, organizations and societies.
Market economy	An economic system in which decisions about costs are guided solely by the service providers and consumers with little government intervention or central planning. This is the opposite of a centrally planned economy, in which government decisions drive most aspects of economic activity.
Mentee	A mentee is the recipient of support, advice and information from a mentor.
Mentor	An experienced and trusted adviser, usually someone who works or who has worked in the field of early years and is able to offer advice and support.
Mentoring	Nurturing of an individual's potential through a supportive relationship with a mentor.
Multi-disciplinary	Relating to, or making use of, several professional disciplines at once.
NPQICL	National Professional Qualification in Integrated Centre Leadership.
Ofsted	Office for Standards in Education.
Parents	Relating to the role described in law – mothers, fathers, carers and all those who have taken on this role in children's lives, either temporarily or as a biological family.
Participatory management	The practice of empowering employees to participate in organizational decision-making.
Partnership with parents	Partnership is distinct from 'involvement'. It characterizes a working relationship based on mutual respect, openness, democracy and sharing information or experiences in order to promote equality

and avoid discriminatory practice for children and their families. It is recognized that an 'ideal' model is proposed and that there may be constraints in some roles or settings to achieving this in practice.

Pedagogy

The science and principles of teaching children based on the characteristics of children as learners.

Post-modernist society

Modernism refers to historical attitudes and beliefs resulting from political and social movements within the 20th century. Post-modernism refers to themes and debates emerging from and superseding these ideas within contemporary society.

Practitioners

The adults who, as 'secondary carers', support children's learning across a range of settings. A person practising a profession – in this case, a person working within the field of early years.

Reflective practice

The art of analysing what has been, how it was done, and why it was done in that way. This analysis is then used to inform future practice.

SEN

Special Educational Needs.

Settings

The range of contexts in which children are the recipients of early childhood services.

Social capital

Making connections with and between social networks to develop shared interests, mutual trust and group collectiveness within a community.

Social cohesion

Different people coming together with willingness to exchange ideas and share experiences to engage in collective participation.

Stakeholders

Interest groups within services, for example, children, parents, practitioners and service providers.

Teams   Teams are groups of practitioners that the leader/manager has contact with on a day-to-day basis. In Integrated Children's Centres, the team will include professionals from various agencies based within the setting, those with whom practitioners work towards a common goal of positive outcomes for the child. Parents can usefully be included in the broad definition of 'team'.

Transactional approach   An approach to understanding behaviour by analysing the 'transactions' or interactions which occur between people.

Transformational leadership   Transformational leaders start with a vision that will excite and convert potential followers. They take opportunities and use effective strategies to lead others towards this vision. This takes dynamism and enthusiasm and, in effect, they are selling themselves as well as the vision.

Value bonds   Developing an ethos which is inclusive of individual needs, group beliefs and leadership ideals.

References

Andrews, M. (2007) *But How Held is The Child? A Children's Centre, Change Leadership and Lessons to be Learned.* Unpublished Masters Dissertation submitted for Master of Arts in Integrated Provision for Children and Families: Pen Green Research, Development and Training Base/University of Leicester.

Argyris, C. (1991) 'Teaching Smart People How to Learn'. *Harvard Business Review.* May/June 69(3): 99–109. web.ebscohost.com (Accessed 17.01.08)

Arnstein, S.R. (1969) 'A Ladder of Citizen Participation'. *Journal of American Planning Association.* 35(4): 124–42. London: Routledge and Kegan Paul.

Atkinson, M., Wilkin, A., Stott, A., Doherty, P. & Kinder, K. (2002) *Multi-Agency Working: A Detailed Study.* Slough: NFER.

Atkinson, M., Kinder, K. & Doherty, P. (2003) *On Track: A Qualitative Study of the Early Impacts of Services.* London: DfES.

Aubrey, C. (2007) *Leading and Managing in the Early Years.* London: Sage.

Baldock, P., Fitzgerald, D. & Kay, J. (2005) *Understanding Early Years Policy.* London: Paul Chapman.

Ball, C. (1994) *Start Right Report: The Importance of Early Learning.* London: Royal Society for the Encouragement of Arts, Manufactures & Commerce.

Bee, H. (2000) *The Developing Child* (9th edn). Boston, MA: Allyn and Bacon.

Begley, P.T. (2001) 'In Pursuit of Authentic School Leadership Practices'. *International Journal of Leadership in Education.* 4(4): 353–65.

Bion, W. (1962) *Learning from Experience.* New York: Basic Books.

Boddy, J., Wigfall, V. & Simon, A. (2006) *Re-discovering Community Social Work? An Evaluation of a Social Worker Based in Children's Centres.* London: Thomas Coram Research Unit, Institute of Education, University of London.

Bottery, M. (2003) 'Uses and Abuses of Quality: The Need for a Civic Version', in Preedy, M., Glatter, R. & Wise, C. (eds) *Strategic Leadership and Educational Improvement.* London: Paul Chapman and Open University Press.

Bruce, T. (2005) *Early Childhood Education.* London: Hodder and Stoughton.

Bruce, T. (2006) *Early Childhood: A Guide for Students.* London: Sage.

Bruner, J. (1990) *Acts of Meaning.* Cambridge, MA: Harvard University Press.

Burleson, W. (2005) *Developing Creativity, Motivation and Self-actualisation with Learning Systems.* Cambridge: Elsevier Ltd.

Callan, S. (2006) 'What is mentoring?', in Robins, A. (ed.) *Mentoring in the Early Years.* London: Sage.

Callan, S. & Copp, E. (2006) 'The mentor as "the one in the middle"', in Robins, A. (ed.) *Mentoring in the Early Years.* London: Sage.

Cameron, A. & Lart, R. (2003) 'Factors Promoting and Obstacles Hindering Joint Working: A Systematic Review of the Research Evidence'. *Journal of Integrated Care.* 11(2): 9–17.

Carlock, C. (1999) *Enhancing Self-esteem* (3rd edn). Philadelphia: Accelerated Development.

Carnall, C. (1991) *Managing Change.* London: Routledge.

Clark, D. (1996) *Schools as Learning Communities: Transforming Education.* London: Cassell.

Claxton, G. (1997) *Hare Brained and Tortoise Mind.* London: Fourth Estate.

Clutterbuck, D. (2004) *Everyone Needs a Mentor: Fostering Talent in Your Organization* (4th edn). London: Chartered Institute of Personnel and Development.

Clutterbuck, D. (2005) *How to Make the Most of Group Mentoring.* Burnham: Clutterbuck Associates.

Coleman, J.S. (1993) 'The Rational Reconstruction of Society'. *American Sociological Review.* 58(1): 1–15.

Colenso, M. (1997) *High Performing Teams.* Oxford: Butterworth-Heinemann.

CWDC (2006) *Early Years Professional National Standards.* London: CWDC.

Dahlberg, G. & Moss, P. (2005) *Ethics and Politics in Early Childhood Education.* London: Routledge.

Dahlberg, G., Moss, P. & Pence, A. (1999) *Beyond Quality in Early Childhood Education and Care: Postmodern Perspectives.* London: Routledge Farmer.

Daly, M., Byers, E. & Taylor, W. (2004) *Early Years Management in Practice.* Oxford: Heinemann.

DCSF (2007) *The Children's Plan – Building Brighter Futures: Summary.* Norwich: TSO.

DEE (1998) *Meeting the Childcare Challenge: A Framework and Consultation Document.* London: HMSO.

Denhardt, R.B., Denhardt, J.V. & Aristigueta, M.P. (2002) *Managing Human Behaviour in Public and Non-Profit Organizations.* London: Sage.

DfES (2000) *Curriculum Guidance for the Foundation Stage.* Sudbury: QCA Publications.

DfES (2002) *Birth to Three Matters: A Framework to Support Children in Their Earliest Years.* Nottingham: DfES.

DfES (2003a) *National Standards for Under 8s Daycare and Childminding.* Nottingham: DfES.

DfES (2003b) *The Impact of Parental Involvement on their Children's Education.* London: DfES/0645/2003.

DfES (2004a) *Every Child Matters: Change for Children.* London: TSO.

DfES (2004b) *Five Year Strategy for Children and Learners.* London: TSO.

DfES (2004c) *Every Child Matters: Next Steps.* London: TSO.

DfES (2004d) *The Children Act.* London: TSO.

DfES (2005a) *The Children's Workforce Strategy.* Nottingham: DfES.

DfES (2005b) *A Sure Start Children's Centre for Every Community, Phase 2 Planning Guidance (2006–08).* London: DfES.

DfES (2005c) *Key Elements of Effective Practice.* London: HMSO.

DfES (2006a) *Children's Workforce Strategy: Building an Integrated Qualifications Framework.* London: TSO.

DfES (2006b) *The Common Assessment Framework for Children and Young People: Managers Guide.* www.everychildmatters.gov.uk/resources and practice/IG00063/ (Accessed 18.12.07)

DfES (2006c) *Common Assessment Framework for Children and Young People: Practitioners Guide.* Nottingham: DfES.

DfES (2007a) *The Early Years Foundation Stage: Setting the Standards for Learning, Development and Care for Children from Birth to Five.* Nottingham: DfES.

DfES (2007b) *Building a World-class Workforce for Children, Young People and Families.* Children's Workforce Strategy Update, Spring. London: TSO.

DfES (2007c) *National Standards for Leaders of Sure Start Children's Centres.* London: TSO.

DfES (2007d) *Every Parent Matters.* Nottingham: DfES.

DfES (2007e) *Statutory Guidance on Making Arrangements to Safeguard and Promote the Welfare of Children under Section 11 of the Children Act 2004.* London: DfES.

DoH/DfES (2004) *The National Service Framework for Children, Young People and Maternity Services.* Executive Summary. London: TSO.

DoH/DfES/The Home Office (2000) *Framework for the Assessment of Children in Need and their Families.* London: HMSO.

Drucker, P.F. (1999) *Management Challenges for the 21st Century.* Oxford: Butterworth-Heinemann.

Duffy, B. & Marshall, J. (2007) 'Leadership in Management Work', in Siraj-Blatchford, I., Clarke, K. & Needham, M. (eds) *The Team Around the Child: Multi-agency Working in the Early Years.* Stoke on Trent: Trentham Books.

Equal Opportunities Commission (2004) *Women Men Different Equal.* Manchester: EOC.

Evans, L. (2003) 'Leadership Role: Morale, Job Satisfaction and Motivation', in Kydd, L., Anderson, L. & Newton, W. (eds) *Leading People and Teams in Education.* London: Paul Chapman and Open University Press.

Foley, P., Roche, K. & Tucker, S. (eds) (2001) *Children in Society.* London: Palgrave.

Fowler, K. & Robins, A. (2006) 'Being Reflective: Encouraging and Teaching Reflective Practice', in Robins, A. (ed.) *Mentoring in the Early Years.* London: Sage.

Friedman, M. (2005) *Trying Hard is Not Good Enough: How to Produce Measurable Improvements for Customers and Communities.* Crewe: Trafford Publishing.

Fullan, M. (1999) *Change Forces: The Sequel.* London: Falmer Press.

Fullan, M. (2004) *Leading in a Culture of Change: A Personal Action Guide and Workbook.* San Francisco: Jossey-Bass.

Fullan, M. (2005) *Leadership and Sustainability.* London: Sage.

Gill, R. (2006) *Theory and Practice of Leadership.* London: Sage.

Goldman, R. (2005) *Fathers' Involvement in their Children's Education.* www.basic-skills.co.uk (Accessed 11.01.08)

Goleman, D. (1996) *Emotional Intelligence: Why Can it Matter More Than IQ?* London: Bloomsbury.

Gross, R. (2005) *Psychology: The Science of Mind and Behaviour* (5th edn). London: Hodder & Stoughton.

Hallam, S., Castle, F. & Rogers, L. (2004) *Research and Evaluation of Behaviour Improvement Programmes: Interim Report.* London: Institute of Education.

Halsey, K., Gulliver, C., Johnson, A., Martin, K. & Kindler, K. (2005) *Evaluation of Behaviour and Education Support Teams.* National Foundation for Educational Research. Research report no. RR706.

Handy, C. (1994) *The Empty Raincoat.* London: Arrow.

Harris, A. & Lambert, L. (2003) *Building Leadership Capacity for School Improvement.* Maidenhead: Open University Press.

Hartman, A. (1978) 'Diagrammatic Assessment of Family Relationships'. *Social Casework.* 57: 65–72.

Hegarty, S. (1993) *Special Needs in Ordinary Schools: An Overview.* London: Cassell.

House of Commons Select Committee on Public Accounts (2007) 38th report prepared 17 July 2007, Section 2, 'Improving local management and governance of children's centres'. www.publications.parliament.uk (Accessed 17.01.08)

James, W. (1890) *Principles of Psychology.* New York: Holt.

Jones, C. & Pound, L. (2008) *Leadership and Management in the Early Years: From Principles to Practice.* Maidenhead: OUP.

Jourard, S.M. (1971) *Self-disclosure: An Experimental Analysis of the Transparent Self.* New York: Wiley Inter-science.

Khan, T. (2005) *Fathers' Involvement in Early Years Settings: Findings From Research: Executive Summary.* London: PLA.

Kubler-Ross, E. (1969) *On Death and Dying.* London: Macmillan.

Kurtz, Z. & James, C. (2002) *What's New: Learning from the CAMHS Innovation Projects.* London: Department of Health.

Laevers, F. (2000) 'Forward to Basics! Deep Level Learning and the Experiential Approach'. *Early Years.* 20(2): 20–9.

Langston, A. (2006) 'Why Parents Matter', in Abbott, L. and Langston, A. (eds) *Parents Matter: Supporting the Birth to Three Matters Framework.* Maidenhead: Open University Press.

Leithwood, K. & Aitken, R. (1995) *Making Schools Smarter: A System for Monitoring School and District Progress.* California: Corwin Press.

Levin, B. (2003) 'Conceptualising Education Reform', in Preedy, M., Glatter, R. & Wise, C. (eds) *Strategic Leadership and Educational Improvement.* London: Paul Chapman and Open University Press.

Lo, R. & Henderson, A. (2007) *The Social Child.* London: PLA.

MacLeod-Brudenell, I. (ed.) (2004) *Advanced Early Years Care and Education.* London: Heinmann.

Martin, C. & Johnson, J. (1992) 'Children's Self-perceptions and Mothers' Beliefs about Development and Competencies', in Sigel, I., McGillicuddy-De Lisi, A. & Goodnow, J. (eds) *Parental Belief Systems: The Psychological Consequences for Children* (2nd edn). New Jersey: Erlbaum Publishers.

Maslow, A. (1968) *Towards a Psychology of Being.* New York: Van Nostrund.

Mathivet, S. & Francis, T. (2007) *Listening Together.* London: PLA.

McClenaghan, P. (2000) 'Social Capital: Exploring the Theoretical Foundations of Community Development Education'. *British Educational Research Journal.* 26(5): 565–82.

McGivney, V. (2000) *The Contribution of Pre-Schools to the Community. A Research Project on the Role of Pre-schools in Tackling Social Inclusion.* London: Pre-School Learning Alliance.

Mekki, A. (2004) 'Overview of Social Welfare', in Wyse, D. (ed.) *Childhood Studies: An Introduction.* London: Blackwell.

Miller, L. & Devereux, J. (2004) *Supporting Children's Learning in the Early Years.* London: David Fulton.

Moore, E. (2007) *Ringing the Changes: The Middle Leader's Role in Leading Change.* Nottingham: NCSL.

Morgan, G. (1986) *Images of Organization.* Thousand Oaks, CA: Sage.

Mortimore, P. (ed.) (1999) *Understanding Pedagogy.* London: Paul Chapman.

Moss, P. (2006) 'Structures, Understandings and Discourses: Possibilities for Re-envisioning the Early Childhood Worker'. *Contemporary Issues in Early Childhood.* 7(1): 30–42.

Moss, P. & Pence, A. (eds) (1994) *Valuing Quality in Early Childhood Services.* London: Paul Chapman.

Moyles, J. (2006) *Effective Leadership and Management in the Early Years.* London: Oxford University Press.

Moyles, J. (ed.) (2007) *Early Years Foundations: Meeting the Challenge.* Maidenhead: OUP.

Mujis, D., Aubrey, C., Harris, A. & Briggs, M. (2004) 'How Do They Manage? A Review of the Research on Leadership in Early Childhood'. *Journal of Early Childhood Research.* 2: 157–71.

Mukherjee, S., Beresford, B. & Sloper, P. (1999) *Key Working: An Analysis of Keyworker Services for Families with Disabled Children.* Bristol: The Policy Press.

Mullins, L.J. (1993) *Management and Organisational Behaviour.* London: Pitman Publishing.

NCSL (2007) 'Children and Families to Benefit as New Professional Standards Announced'. www.ncsl.or.uk/aboutus/pressreleases (Accessed 01.10.07)

NFER (2006) *National Evaluation of On Track, Phase Two Tracking Service Users: On Track in Practice.* Policy Research Bureau. Slough: NFER.

NQIN (2007) *Quality Improvement Principles.* London: National Children's Bureau.

Nutbrown, C. (2006) *Key Concepts in Early Childhood Education.* London: Sage.

Obholzer, A. & Zagier Roberts, V. (eds) (1994) *The Unconscious at Work: Individual and Organisational Stress in the Human Services.* London: Routledge.

Ofsted (2006) *Are you Ready for Your Inspection?* London: HMI.

Parsloe, E. & Wray, M. (2000) *Coaching and Mentoring: Practical Methods to Improve Learning.* London: Kogan Page.

Percy-Smith, J. (2005) *What Works in Strategic Partnerships for Children?* Essex: Barnardos.

Pettit, B. (2003) *Effective Joint Working between CAMHS and Schools.* Research report, Department for Children Schools and Families. www.dfes.gov.uk/research/data/uploadfiles/RB412.pdf (Accessed 18.12.07)

Piaget, J. (1977) *The Development of Thought, Equilibrium and Cognitive Structures.* New York: Viking Press.

Pound, L. (2005) *How Children Learn.* Leamington Spa: Step Forward Publishing.

Pugh, G. & De'Ath, E. (1989) *Working Towards Partnership in the Early Years.* London: National Children's Bureau.

Quinton, D. (2004) *Supporting Parents: Messages from Research.* London: Jessica Kingsley.

Ringer, M. (2002) *Group Action: The Dynamics of Groups in Therapeutic, Educational and Corporate Settings.* London: Jessica Kingsley.

Robins, A. (ed.) (2006) *Mentoring in the Early Years*. London: Sage.

Rodd, J. (2006) *Leadership in Early Childhood* (3rd edn). Buckingham: OUP.

Rogers, C. (1983) *Freedom to Learn for the 1980s*. Columbus: Merrill.

Rogers, N. (2006) *Author, Artist, Therapist/Facilitator*. www.nrogers.com (Accessed 15.11.07)

Rogoff, B. (1990) *Apprenticeship in Thinking*. London: Oxford University Press.

Rogoff, B. (2003) *The Cultural Nature of Human Development*. Oxford: Oxford University Press.

Schaffer, R. (1996) *Social Development*. London: Blackwell Publishing.

Schein, E. (1985) *Organizational Culture and Leadership*. San Francisco: Jossey-Bass.

Seel, R. (2007) www.new-paradigm.co.uk/richardseel.htm (Accessed 02.12.07)

Sergiovanni, T.J. (2001) *Leadership: What's in it for Schools?* London: Routledge Falmer.

Sloper, P. (2004) 'Facilitators and Barriers for Co-ordinated Multi-agency Services in Child Care'. *Health and Development*. 30(6): 571–80.

Smith, A. & Langston, A. (1999) *Managing Staff in the Early Years*. London: Routledge.

Smith, M.K. (2001) 'Kurt Lewin Groups, Experiential Learning and Action Research'. www.infed.org/thinkers/et-lewin (Accessed 18.12.07)

Smith, R. (2005) *Values and Practice in Children's Services*. Basingstoke: Palgrave Macmillan.

Snyder, M. (1974) 'Self-monitoring of Expressive Behaviour'. *Journal of Personality and Social Psychology*. 30(4): 526–37.

Snyder, M. (1987) *Public Appearance/Private Realities: The Psychology of Self-Monitoring*. New York: W.H. Freeman.

Stephenson, R. (2006) 'Promoting Self Expression Through Art Therapy'. *Generations*. 30(1): 24–6.

Stokes, J. (1994) 'Institutional Chaos and Personal Stress', in Obholzer, A. & Roberts Zagier, V. (eds) *The Unconscious at Work: Individual and Organisational Stress in the Human Services*. London: Routledge.

Sure Start (2005) *Research to Inform the Management and Governance of Children's Centres*. London: Sure Start.

SWAP (2007) *SWAP*. Social Policy and Social Work Subject Centre, Higher Education Academy, School of Social Sciences, University of Southampton. www.swap.ac.uk (Accessed 18.12.07)

The Childcare Act (2006) *Childcare Act*. London: TSO. www.opsi.gov.uk/acts/acts2006 (Accessed 18.12.07)

The Children Act (1989) www.opsi.gov.uk/acts (Accessed 20.12.07)

The General Social Care Council (2007). *A Joint Statement*. The General Social Care Council (GSCC), The General Teaching Council for England (GTC) and the Nursing and Midwifery Council (NMC). London: GSCC.

The Scottish Government (2005) *Getting it Right for Every Child: Proposals for Action*. www.scotland.gov.uk/Publications/2005/06/20135608/56173 (Accessed 18.12.07)

Together for Children (2008) *Toolkit for Reaching Priority and Excluded Families*. Birmingham: Together for Children.

Vincent, C. (1996) *Parents and Teachers: Power and Participation*. London: Falmer Press.

Whalley, M. (1994) *Learning to be Strong: Setting up a Neighbourhood Service for Under-fives and their Families.* London: Hodder & Stoughton.

Whalley, M. (and the Pen Green Centre Team) (1997) *Working with Parents.* London: Hodder & Stoughton.

Whalley, M. (and the Pen Green Centre Team) (2001) *Involving Parents in their Children's Learning.* London: Paul Chapman.

Whalley, M. (and the Pen Green Centre Team) (2007) *Involving Parents in their Children's Learning* (2nd edn). London: Paul Chapman.

Wilson, V. & Pirric, A. (2000) *Multidisciplinary Team Working: Beyond the Barriers? A Review of Issues.* Scottish Council for Research in Education.

Winnicott, D.W. (1971) *Playing and Reality.* Abingdon: Routledge.

Yorkshire & Humber Children's Fund (2004) 'Making the Case for Prevention'. www.everychildmatters.gov.uk/deliveringservices/multiagencyworking/benefi tsofmultiagency/ (Accessed 14.03.08)

Index

Added to a page number 'f' denotes a figure and 't' denotes a table

DATE DUE